Unchained

Breaking Through Barriers
(Empowerment for Incarcerated Women)

By
C. Williams

-Acknowledgements

I dedicate my very first book to my daughter. LaChelle, you are the love of my life, the beat in my heart, my Blessing from God and my inspiration for which I have arrived to receive and walk in the purpose planned for my life. I realize and accept that all was not pleasant throughout your childhood, and you've encountered some experiences that were less favorable. Thank you for your unconditional love and forgiveness which created an endless fire to always be a better mother and a woman. You are a beautiful, creative, and compassionate young woman who will do great things in your life because of those experiences. For you LaChelle, I create this as an everlasting token of my love for you to hold in your heart as you journey to accept and fulfill your purpose in life.

I want to thank all of the ladies who take my women empowerment workshops in Hampton Roads Regional Jail, Virginia Peninsula Regional Jail and Western Tidewater Regional Jail. You ladies are the reason WE1A continues to exist. Your desire to become unchained from your past and enter into your now lives blesses my heart. I know it's not always easy for you to address your most deeply rooted pains, especially in front of a group of women you don't know. But you persevere through the pain in order to release it. I'm so very proud of all of you. Continue to walk in your truth so the light of your healing will shine. I love you, I believe in you and I pray for nothing but the best for you, in all you do.

To my phenomenal WE1A facilitators, I thank you for your dedication to sow into the ladies who attend the empowerment groups in the correctional facilities. You are such major contributors to the growth of the organization. You are my missing pieces of the puzzle which puts it all together. I am so very grateful to you all.

To my brother Kenny, whose unconditional love keeps me motivated and grounded. Your confidence in me, unwavering support, straight-no-chaser advice and reality checks keep me balanced. I love you.

Thank you MJ McGlen for seeing in me what you felt would be such a fantastic and exciting experience for WE1A and my journey. You saw it through hearing my passion for my prison ministry. Your enthusiasm for where your spirit sees WE1A in the future is priceless to me.

Table of Contents

Introduction

What a truly exciting and grateful journey I've begun. April 11, 2014 was the date of the first women empowerment group in Newport News City Jail in Newport News, VA.

Everything happens for a reason. As we journey each encounter of our lives, there are lessons and a preparation within each one. Some are experienced for longer periods of time than others. Without the necessary tools to empower ourselves, it can prolong the process and make it extremely difficult to not face it head on, but also challenging to move forward. When the pain becomes unbearable, we're forced to make a decision regarding what we are going to do with that pain. We just want it to go away and however temporary it may be; we suppress it with what we know to use or what we may possibly be introduced to. Every reaction will create either an effective or consequential result. This has become a repeated routine for so many and our first "rock-bottom" is not always the finale.

The following essays incorporate a few of the assigned essays that were designed for incarcerated women to begin their journey of healing. I, however; had never answered them. I am always very supportive of the pain shared by the women because it was so familiar since I had experienced it and I was able to identify their brokenness. I challenge anyone who reads this book to identify within yourself whether you have any relevant circumstances to some of the essays to complete the process the women do; think about it, write it down, commit to releasing it after reading it aloud to hear yourself saying it. The women read aloud to not only release it, but to sow into and liberate the other women in the group who are experiencing a struggle with the process. They support and empower one another while creating a Sisterhood within the group and within the pods to which they're assigned. Some of the women remain in contact with one another when they're released. They fought through the pain together and served as a support system to one another.

For every incarcerated woman who decides to complete any of the essays for your own personal

Unchained

growth, please know and accept that not everyone will be able to identify nor have compassion for what you have been through. When people have not experienced what you have and they've lived a different kind of life, they can sometimes make light of your situation as though it shouldn't be hard to move forward. You cannot teach or force anyone to understand what you've been through. You can't teach them to feel the difficulty you experienced. We live in a society that is so judgmental and you'll encounter many individuals and organizations who don't believe in 2nd chances. Many have a perception that once a criminal, always a criminal. You will have more doors slammed in your face than you will have opened for a chance of redemption. People are going to be who they are and they will never change unless they choose to do so.

You have a challenge ahead of you, commit that giving up is not an option. Surround yourself or create a support system of individuals where you are able to lift each other up when you feel you're facing tricks of the enemy. Keep the God of your understanding up front and center in all you think and do. You must not give in to negative societal entities, but you must do your part. Don't spend time trying to detour your storm by going around it, over it or under it. Go straight through it and victory shall surely be yours. Your first, and sometimes your most difficult decision can be accepting that you deserve to live a life of forgiveness, wholeness and peace. Your second, making the choice to become unchained from your old self and your past. Do your work and receive the reward. You are worthy, God says so. If no one has told you today.... I love you, I believe in you and I pray the very best for you, in all you do.

Amen

Whenever you find yourself doubting how far you can go, just remember how far you have come.
Remember, everything you have faced,
all the battles you have won,
and all the fears you have overcome.

Unchained

DAY 1

You can accept or reject the way you are treated by other people,
but until you heal the wounds of your past, you will continue to bleed. You can bandage the bleeding with food, with alcohol,
with drugs, with work, with cigarettes, with sex, but eventually, it will all ooze through and stain your life.
You must find the strength to open the wounds, stick your hands inside, pull out the core of the pain that is holding you in your past, the memories,
and make peace with them.
~Iyanla Vanzant

My Truth, My Freedom

The truth will always make you free.
John 8:31-47

The truth is most often used to mean being in accord with fact or reality, or fidelity to an original or standard.

Freedom is the absence of necessity, coercion, or constraint in choice or action.

For every step we take in an effort to move forward with our lives, we must make in truth. To be absent or in denial of what is true, especially about ourselves will more likely than not cause us to move in directions that are not most beneficial to and for us.

Not just ourselves, but for the people around us who love us and depend on us. It can be an extremely difficult task to move forward when we do not accept what is true. We must find a way to make a commitment to want to not only feel better about everyday life, but a commitment to unchain ourselves from the experiences which leave a continuous absence of internal and external freedom.

If you are bearing the emotional attachment to, let's say childhood molestation; the feelings associated with that type of violation can cause a downward spiral effect if not addressed with interventions that create a healthy thought process. What we're exposed to and engaged in at an early age majorly contributes to how our mindset develops. The way we think, how we interact with others and how we feel about ourselves.

Personal Reflection:

How in the world did I manage to marry the same type of men with similar characteristics as the man who molested me for eight years of my life? At 8 years old I was so impressionable and what I was exposed to, I

Unchained

knew. What I knew, I used. I learned to manipulate to get what I wanted, to get out of receiving a punishment. If I let him touch this or that, I'd get what I wanted. Looking back when I began to heal and rid myself of the guilt, shame and embarrassment, I was trying to figure out how and why it happened. It did make me feel a sense of being special. Like it was a boyfriend/girlfriend relationship between a little girl and a grown man. That's what he wanted it to feel like. A man whose position was to be a stepfather, a leader in the home and a provider. The line was crossed with the utmost inappropriate intimacy and control. When I turned sixteen years old, I was able to date. I started dating boys, but they were not as fascinating to me as a grown man was, I only knew a grown man. I began dating grown men. My maturity level was a bit higher than girls my own age due to being put in a woman's role of intimacy. Those relationships were short lived because I refused to have intercourse with any of them. I was never talked to about birth control so I was not only afraid of getting pregnant, but I feared what everyone would say since my mother had me at fifteen years old. I felt like I had already beaten the odds because I was sixteen. I had become interested in different people and they had begun calling regularly. That was always a problem with the step-father, I just wanted him to leave me alone. It seemed like every opportunity possible, I was on punishment and couldn't receive any phone calls and couldn't go out. When I was able to go out, the guy had to come inside the house and go through this interrogation which seemed like forever. I'm surprised anyone still wanted to take me out. It was so ridiculous and excessive. I remember this one guy asked me, "What was up with all of that, we're just going to the movies?" I never said anything. I was so embarrassed and I often thought someone would find out what he had been doing. When I'd return, there were what seemed like a thousand questions. I didn't know how to deal with that. After a short while I would just begin to sit in my room and my feelings were becoming so overwhelming, I thought I'd never get out of this situation. Who was I going to tell? I sat on the edge of the bed one night with a razor blade. I was trying to figure out how to best slit my wrist. I just wanted to gradually fall asleep and bleed to death, but I had a low tolerance to pain. In my

Unchained

mind, I thought if I started midway of my arm with a couple of small, quick slits, I could build up a tolerance and my intention was to work my way down until I could just clip that main vein and I'd be successful. Evidently, it wasn't a successful attempt because I'm sitting here writing about it. After 35 years, I can still see a couple of the faint marks on my inner arm.

The truth about what was going on in my home came out when I was seventeen. I had been dating LM, and refused to stop seeing him. If my step-father and I had an altercation, I would run away from home and call him. He'd pick me up somewhere and we'd be together. This one particular time when I returned home, all hell broke loose. We were arguing and before I knew it, this man had hit me. He hit me so hard that my mother had to take me to the hospital. It was at the hospital that the truth came out about how and why it was happening. I was immediately put in a foster home. A foster home at seventeen years old! There were never any charges against him, no arrest, no court appearances, nothing that I've ever known of.

My mother would go on to marry this man and have two children with him. Later I found out this man was a heroin addict and an alcoholic. They broke up some time later and I believe that he'd been hit by a car a couple of times on different occasions while out drunk and eventually ended up dying. I went to the funeral to support my mother and when we were all walking up to view the body, I remember my mother kissing him before she passed by. I was behind her and I was following suit, but when I bent over to kiss him as well, something felt like it jerked my entire body back and I couldn't do it. I was saying to myself, "I really can't stand you and I'm glad you're out of my life forever!" I just walked away and sat down feeling a sense of relief. I had no remorse and I wasn't even close to being sad as a result of what he had done to me since I was eight years old. And even though the molestation was no longer occurring, that seed had already been planted.

I remained in that foster home until I graduated Ross High School in Brentwood, New York. Afterwards, I moved to my grandparents' home and got a job.

Somehow LM and I eventually began seeing one another again, I went on to marry him at 18 years old and he was 28. We eloped to Atlantic City, New Jersey. He was a truck driver and drove cross-country. I rode with him for about 3 or 4 months and had been to all states except three. I've been to places I never thought I would. There were abusive behaviors during that time on the road together which were displayed. No knowledge or insight of what those behaviors would eventually turn out to be nearly cost me my life.

I became pregnant in June of 1985 while we lived in Newport News, VA, but moved back to New York a few months later. We stayed with one of my aunts, but that didn't work out well. He was so abusive during my pregnancy. We constantly fought throughout the nine months. I eventually moved back to my grandparents' home. My daughter was born in March of 1986. She was our first and only child. I remember seeing my grandfather looking in the baby unit and having such a proud look on his face. My grandmother was so instrumental during those first few months. This was her 1st great-grandchild and she knew exactly what to do, because I sure didn't. When my daughter had colic, she cried so much. I recall one night I was so tired, my grandmother was sitting in the living room and told me to bring the baby to her. My grandmother tightly wrapped a receiving blanket around her stomach and shortly afterwards she went right to sleep.

LM and I were always breaking up and making up the entire time we were married. We eventually ended up moving to Bridgeport, Connecticut, where we lived together for a while. Although he was still driving on the road, whenever he came home there was always something to fight about. My daughter was approaching 5 years old. I was so sick and tired of fighting with him. Many times in the past, when we had a fight, he would go on the road and I would have moved out before he came back. This one particular time, a conversation took place. I made the decision that I no longer wanted my daughter to continue seeing this type of behavior growing up. I felt like she would end up in the same type of relationship, just as I did and I didn't want that for her. The conversation seemed like there was understanding

Unchained

and a mutual understanding, NOT! He went back on the road and I would be gone before he returned. As I was packing up our things, I found a steak knife in between the mattress and box spring. I wondered if he was planning to stab me in my sleep. I moved into my own apartment with my daughter and a few weeks went by before he and I spoke to one another. I didn't tell him where I lived because I just didn't want a problem. I didn't stop him from seeing my daughter, I just preferred to meet him somewhere. We eventually spoke and he said he wanted to give me some money to get my daughter some summer clothes. I remember him calling me into the late hours of the night and he wanted me to come out and meet him somewhere. One of my friends had her two youngest children staying the night with my daughter and I couldn't leave the house, even if I wanted to meet him, although I had no desire to. He still at this point didn't know where I lived, I assumed. Little to my surprise, he showed up at my door at 8:30am on a Sunday morning. He had sunglasses on and looked very suspicious. I didn't want to let him because the kids were asleep and I figured more than likely we were going to be arguing. I held my foot at the bottom of the door so he wouldn't push his way in, but he did anyway. He pushed me against the wall and was making statements of some kind that I don't really recall. The knife appeared and he held it to my throat. I found myself bargaining because I didn't want to awaken the kids, nor did I want any of them to see what was about to happen. I tried to get him to calm down and before I knew it, he stabbed me in the neck. He pulled the knife back and attempted to do it again. I remember grabbing the knife and he snatched it from my hand. My fingers were cut in numerous places, but he managed to stab me again and in the very same area.

As nosey as my neighbors were any other time and with all the screaming that was going on, not a single person came to the door. I fell to the floor because I was having difficulty breathing and I couldn't scream anymore. I surely thought this was it. I laid on the floor and while trying to gasp for breath, I found myself looking for the light I had heard people looking for when they're getting ready to die. Well, the light never came. I suddenly heard the kids screaming and crying and decided to get up and go back into the

Unchained

apartment. There was blood everywhere, my clothes were drenched with blood and it seemed blood was just pouring out of my neck. I wasn't sure exactly what to do, but I was trying to dial 911 and call my friend to get the kids and the blood kept pouring over the buttons on the phone, I asked one of the kids to dial 911. Someone called 911 because I heard them coming. I was still pretty conscience, but it seemed I was a little delirious because I wanted to change my clothes, wash my face and brush my teeth before they got there. When I went to brush my teeth, the water came out through my neck and it stung so badly that I stopped and just kept trying the wash thc blood up. The last thing I recall about that day was my name being asked in the hospital and people kept asking me my name and my age. It had become so repetitious and I was getting irritated because I started to not remember what I last said, and asked the final person to ask the person that last asked me because I just told them. I didn't know what I was saying. The next thing to happen is beyond me. LM ran off after he stabbed me and basically left me there to die. I'm not sure whether he turned himself in or what, but he did go to jail.

I was in ICU and my mother and one my aunts came to see me. My friend whose children was spending the night brought them to see me to show them I was ok because her youngest son thought I had died. My baby was young, but oh so sweet. She brought this little picture of her and me and put it on the bedside table. I was so grateful my friend brought them there to see I was still alive. The situation was traumatic enough and maybe she thought it would ease any worry they may have had.

After I moved to a hospital room, someone from social services came to see me and asked me a lot of questions. They signed me up for Medicaid, financial assistance and food stamps. They paid my hospital bills and what a load that was off of me. I didn't have any health insurance and the transition was going to be hard enough.

There were programs I could sign up for once I got out of the hospital and was able to get around well enough. One of the programs helped me get some additional training, they paid for my daycare and gave me bus tickets to get back and forth to the program. I received Social Services assistance for 6 months and took full advantage of the opportunity to get back on my feet. People were so nasty when I had to go and cash my state check. When I used food stamps, we had the paper one's back then, people looked at me very judgingly. I couldn't wait to get off the assistance because of how it made me feel. I never wanted to experience a situation like that again. Don't get me wrong, I was grateful it was there when I needed it, but a drive came over me to do whatever I had to do to prevent me from ever getting on it again. I ended up getting a better job and making more money than I was prior to the incident.

The feelings associated with it were still present and growing. It showed up in my relationships, in the men I chose. I was wearing that abuse, which in turn, attracted various other abusive men. It was never psychologically addressed and I never really talked about it much back then. Just going through everyday life with it lurking around me for an opportunity to be taken advantage of.

My truth is that the development of my unhealthy way of thinking began at eight years old. My understanding of life had excelled since I accepted that this was a major factor in the formation of my upbringing and mindset. The true healing and release of the emotions associated with what I went through began when I stopped blaming myself for what occurred. The ways that I've hurt people with my actions, which definitely was not intentional, but something that I learned and grew up with. I refuse to beat myself up about it, and I also refuse to allow anyone to make me feel like I should be ashamed for a situation that began in the life of an eight-year-old girl with a grown man who should have known better, but didn't. Till this day, there continues to be a couple of people in my family who feel I knew exactly what I was doing and consider that to be "just who I am". Those are people who have issues themselves, but refuse to accept, address and step out of it in order to make themselves mentally healthy. I refuse to accept that I have to spend a moment explaining to anyone what child abuse of a sexual nature is who believes that about me. It does illustrate how deep the abuse dwells in my family to even have that type of mindset.

I've chosen to not remain silent in regard to how my childhood was, the many occurrences with what happened to me, but how it affected various areas of my entire life and the capability of making healthy decisions especially where relationships were concerned. My silence decelerated the intensification of my becoming a better person. I use what I've survived during my life to sow into other women who have experienced the same or similar pasts.

I pray for my family because I know the pain runs deep. So many of the women in my family have never been empowered. Their self-esteem is low and that brings forth the envy and animosity towards one another. There was no platform for them to put those issues on the table and talk about how they felt and how it has affected them. My grandmother didn't know it, so how could she sow it into them. There were insults, ridicule, degrading comments and a lack of communication which caused some of the women in my family to bring children into the world and not know how to instill certain traits into them. They can't because they've never known how. They are and have been carrying all that pain for so many years. You can see it so clearly in the interactions that lack within the family. What's not realized is that the longer they refuse to address it, the deeper that pain goes, the harder it is to pull up, the further separated we become.

What are the traumatic experiences that have occurred in your life since childhood that were major contributors to your mindset? It's time to internally invest in YOU. The journey to forgiveness begins when you are able to go to your past to see where the breakdown began, so you'll know where to start. In order to reach an end of being affected emotionally, there has to be a beginning point for your journey. It's at that point which will allow you to see, your current mindset isn't all your fault. Your internal freedom will no longer be concealed as you release it.

My Prayer for you:

May you release any toxicity you are harboring within yourself towards anyone who has caused you harm. Love is love and if you have a healthy mindset, it's easier to accept people for who they are without being judgmental towards them. You can choose to not engage. Love isn't supposed to hurt. I pray you receive how much more peaceful you can be within yourself in your everyday when you choose to love and not hate. I pray you choose to live a functional lifestyle as opposed to adapting to dysfunction that may be around you. I pray that you explode with courage to face your past. I pray it happens right now! Your past is the prelude to your purpose. May you find the freedom within yourself by acknowledging and accepting your truth.

DAY 2

You are not what you have done, but what you have overcome.
All the hardships. All the mistakes. All the rejections.
All the pain.
All the times you questioned why. All of these things have given birth to the wisdom and strength that will help you shine your light on the world,
even in the darkest of hours.
~Unknown Author

Self-Forgiveness

I do not consider that I have made it my own. But one thing I do: forgetting what lies behind and straining forward to what lies ahead.
Philippians 3:13

Self is a person's essential being that distinguishes them from others.

Forgiveness is compassionate feelings that support a willingness to forgive
Or the act of excusing a mistake or offense.

It's amazing how we can take ownership of circumstances we've encountered that were done to us by another person or other people, as well as those things we lacked in our lives at very young ages. We then assume a sole mental responsibility for them. They become rooted within us. This causes all of the feelings and lack thereof associated with those circumstances to grow and spread out. Loosening that root is done by the way we think, thus follows the behaviors or acts. When you steal, fight, disrespect or even kill someone, it's due to that root within you. There is an obstruction which prevents the love in you from sprouting out; not only towards others, but for yourself. As long as the root remains and is shaken or loosened, it will grow. You must completely pull the root out in order for it to stop growing. You can no longer allow the root to feel it's in good ground because it will not die, it doesn't feel there's a need to. You are feeding it with what it wants, what it feels it needs to have and your end result is the growth. The growth of negativity and unproductiveness only increases the already planted seeds of a low self-worth, emptiness, violation and sadness.

Personal Reflection:
I was always a chunky little girl. I was in a car accident when I was younger, back when the dashboards in Chevy's were metal. I had hit the dashboard and it knocked one of my front teeth down my throat. For a long time growing up, I rarely

smiled, showing my teeth since I was missing one. So, being overweight, flat-chested and missing a tooth, was a crazy combo for me. When no one sows into you that you are beautiful just as you are or tells you that you will do great things in your life, you can grow up feeling ugly and worthless. These emotions created a fear in and of myself, and increased a low self-worth. I did not know what loving myself consisted of. I didn't understand self-respect and respect for others. I wasn't taught that. I knew manipulation, and that's what I used to get what I wanted. I was so mean, even to my mother and brother. I was fighting a lot in school, I was angry, unhappy and I talked about other people because I felt so ugly inside. I felt like I could take the focus off of myself and all that I lacked by putting a focus on someone else. The behaviors I exhibited made me feel like I was empty of goodness. I felt I didn't matter to anyone and when I did matter, it was only for them to get something from me or be abusive to me.

I had become so unhappy, not having any purpose and simply existing. I was just tired. Tired of feeling like a failure in relationships, as a wife, a mother, a sister, and a daughter combined with not having any value of or in life.

There were many years before I understood I could ask a higher power for help. My spirit was uplifted when I started to feed my spirit with good things. I began to feel better about the day, each day. The thoughts of taking what I thought was "my life" turned around. I was still not aware of my purpose in this life, but eventually it came. I had to first accept that the destiny for my life would not prevail if I wasn't in it to bring it to fruition.

It was a necessity for me to self-forgive in order to move forward. To detach myself from feeling like everything was all my fault and mine alone. I had to accept that this life had more to offer me than pain and resentment. To free myself of holding onto the way that people felt and thought about me. I also had to commit to do something about it. I refused to be held responsible for feelings that other people had towards me when I was not living the life I was supposed to, and it took a while for me to receive I was supposed to go through all of that in order for me to walk in who I was destined to be. I vowed to no longer be a victim, but victorious over my past circumstances by being a better person. It was a process and not one that would come easily. You can accept and decide to do something different, but that journey will be one where you face daily challenges. You have to keep going. You cannot give up or give in. It's a fight worth facing with a rewarding outcome. You must believe that you are worthy of a crown.

In the beginning, my low self-esteem caused me to feel useless. It brought about all of the negativity I brought to my life. After many years of suffering through life and not having a mental comprehension that I could choose at any moment to change it around. I could choose to not people please as well as not allow others to label me. I could refuse to accept bad behavior of others. I chose to flip it in my favor.

What circumstances do you feel responsible for that sow negativity into your being? What do you need to unchain yourself from so that you can move forward? We cannot hold onto everything that happens to us.

Once you loosen the grip of mental defeat, it makes room for you to receive what your next move is. Your self-esteem will make you choose or release from your life.

My Prayer for you:
I pray that you find forgiveness within yourself and loose those things that do not prosper you. I pray you become engrossed with comfort during and after any overwhelming emotions experienced throughout your self-forgiveness process. May internal freedom find you during this purging while awakening the real you and all that you are meant to be. I pray you, leave your past behind while moving forward. May you release the heaviness which slows you down. Love yourself because you are truly a beautiful being awaiting emergence for an opportunity to sow your good seeds into others.

Amen

DAY 3

Letting go means to come to the realization that some people are a part of your history, but not a part of your destiny.
~Steve Maraboli

A Letter to my Father

Train up a child in the way he should go: and when he is old, he will not depart from it.
Proverbs 22:6

Letter: A direct or personal written or printed message addressed to a person or organization

Father: A male parent

For many women who are fatherless, there's that "little girl" inside of them who wishes so badly that he was there. Wishing he had been there when she needed him the most. We go throughout our lives with a void which we are constantly trying to fill with entities that will never fit. We actually end up causing more pain for ourselves. Additional pain continues to be compounded by the existing pain because what we try to fit into those voids which not only doesn't belong there, but causes its forced entry to eventually fall out. As those feelings become more intense, the further we begin to search, accept and receive those things which will never replace what our original emptiness was. Although a man can contribute to the creation of a life, it takes a real man to accept the role of a father and fulfill the responsibility in which he was intended to sow into that life.

Personal Reflection:

How wonderful it may have been for me to be able to know, and say, "My Daddy". I've sometimes wondered how my life would have turned out had I known you. I don't know why I have no knowledge of you, speculation but no validity. I've spent a long time believing that another man was my father. Since I was three years old, he was all I had known as Dad. I found out different during the repast of a grandfather whom I thought was my biological. Several of us were sitting at the dining room table, and the girlfriend of whom I thought was my father asked me, "Did your mother ever tell you that (we'll call him Mr. X) was not your real father?" I was around fourteen or fifteen years old, full of anger, in a dysfunctional home with a low self-esteem. I immediately called my mother because I was totally stricken with confusion, hurt, disbelief and even angry at my mother for allowing me to find out through this woman, and at a funeral for that matter. I was angry at the fact that my mother never told me.

Wow!! I was almost lost for words beginning to write this. I've never written down any feelings regarding this topic. Even when my participants read this particular assignment in the group about themselves, I've had some feelings about it, but never really put that much "thought" into it other than to share that I've had a similar situation. I would simply say, "I didn't know who my father was either." But in the pursuit of creating a platform for other readers to seek within themselves, any feelings from their pasts that may be presently affecting their lives; it's now time to put my voice to it.

I needed that father figure in my life, I mean, I really needed him. The positive male role model who was supposed to instill those things that would've made me well rounded a lot sooner than what it took me to get there. I needed him to assist in my upbringing, my healthy and functional development as a woman from a man's perspective, a father's point of view to his daughter and the type of man I should accept into my life and the type to deny. Instead, I received, the lack thereof. I needed you to be proud of me for doing something well and something worthy of being praised for as your little girl. I needed to be a little girl, but that was taken away from me without regard to how it would drastically affect my future. I needed you to help raise me and instill values and morals in me, even if you and my mother didn't get along. I know she was young, but evidently she wasn't too young at that particular moment when I was conceived. There was a void in my life filled with lies, deceit and abuse. All of that shadowed me into my adult years with personal relationships and other interactions with people. There was an emptiness that I was filling with all kinds of inappropriate entities. I just needed to be loved by you, a father's love. I needed you to show me what love was. How to give it and how to receive it. I was in search of love from a man to validate me in some way, but instead, predators saw that emptiness and lack of strength to violate my innocence for their perverted and unstable sclf-gain.

It was a long walk into who I am today, and without you. I don't hate you. I don't possess the capacity to hate anyone. I wondered sometimes if you even knew that I existed. I've asked myself, "Did you even know I was here?" Are you still alive? You might not be. What would I do about it if you were? I don't have a desire to do anything about it, because I've chosen me, me without you. The current space I'm in won't allow me to look nor lean back. You are an invisible memory of my past and I've accepted that no one thought I was important enough to not only know any history of you, but even your name. There's no room for you in my present or in my future even if I were to find out who you are. My faith just keeps moving me forward to bigger and better things. Even if you knew I existed and you chose to not be a part of my life, sadly it's a great loss for you. With everything I've endured thus far, I have acknowledged and accepted God and His purpose for my life and you can't even claim any credit for sowing into it. You'll never be able to share in any of the future accomplishments and celebrations of my life. You've missed fifty-one years. There are more years behind me than in front of me and I've chosen to use the remainder of my years to empower other women who are struggling with a similar brokenness. Many of them struggle with no positive male role model in their lives. In any and every way that I can, I am going to lift them up so they can begin to live their lives to the fullest by becoming unchained from the feelings associated with the brokenness. I survived it and I'm better for it, they too will be.

You would be proud of the woman I am today. I'm doing positive things in my life, despite what I've been through. I don't have a bunch of children with different fathers that I couldn't take care of. I still believe in love and I do love. I even love you, whomever and wherever you are. Without your participation to some minute degree, I wouldn't be here.

God's grace and mercy have kept me here. In actuality, I've accepted a Father who will always be within my being, He'll never leave me and can't not acknowledge me since He is my Creator. I believe everything happens for a reason. Whether I understand that reason or not, I've positioned myself to not question it, I simply trust it. I believe those things that don't kill us, make us kill ourselves or kill someone else, makes us stronger. I am stronger and I'm so very thankful for it.

My Prayer for you:
For anyone who has not had a relationship with their biological father, I send up prayers of comfort and strength for you. To anyone who has experienced and endured consequences due to the void in your life that stems from not having a positive male role model in your life, I send up prayers for peace and forgiveness within you. We cannot focus on what we lacked in our lives as a guide to engage in acts of self-destruction and consequential ramifications, but what we can accept is, although things didn't turn out the way we feel they should have, all hope is not lost. You too can choose you and not your circumstances!

Amen

DAY 4

What I wish my Mother would have taught me

Behold, children are a heritage from the Lord, the fruit of the womb a reward.
Psalm 127:3

Mother: a female parent

Taught: to impart knowledge or skill; give instruction

My life seems to have been trial and error to the fifth power. I made so many bad decisions in my life, yet, I'm still here. In this life trying not so much to correct all the wrongs, but to begin again and start by being an overall better person and a better mother, which is what I have left. I must dedicate to celebrate being a better mother, because the issues my daughter and I have had was nothing short of being a divine intervention in the way we've grown; individually and collectively. God had his hand all in that one. I didn't know how to be a mother. I'm not ashamed to say that, because it was true. I won't lie to you and portray to now be this woman who knows it all. In order for you to be able to teach someone else something, you've had to have had it taught to you. You had to have had some verbal and or visual instruction or demonstration. I was married and we discussed and planned to have a child. There was no preparation for mental and emotional growth or stability in that child. I didn't have the knowledge or tools to provide it to her. Time and a host of dysfunctional situations had lapsed before I had finally knew how to. I had some instinct, but lacked pertinent knowledge on what I needed to sow into her as a little girl to follow her into womanhood. I wasn't really shown how to grow into being a woman, so what additional guidance could I give her.

Personal Reflection:
There are moments in a little girl's life where her only desire is her mothers' presence. A daughters' mother is the very first example of a woman a daughter has. It's where she should learn how to care for and carry herself, as well as how to do those things that will lead her into being a woman. When I started my menstrual cycle, I thought I was prepared to take care

of it because when I was in school, we had health education where the girls were taught what to do when it came. The teacher demonstrated what to do with the menstrual pad. So the day arrived, and it was here. I told my mother and she told me where the pads were. I went into the bathroom and this particular pad had an adhesive strip on it, we didn't learn about that kind. I remember looking at it strangely, because I didn't know what to do with it. I said to myself, "How is this thing supposed to stay in place?" Well, four pairs of pants and about an hour later prompted me to confront my mother and tell her I keep staining my pants every few minutes after I sat down. The end result was that I had been putting the pad on wrong. I figured I was supposed to put the sticky part on the hair so it would stick and not move. It was the most painful experience, having to pull that pad off of me. I would have preferred she'd come into the bathroom with me and tell me how to put it on, but it didn't happen that way. There was nothing special about the experience of that happening and there really wasn't much to follow afterwards. I vividly remember that specific incident and vowed when my daughter began hers, it was going to be celebrated. It's a major turning point in a girl's life and when my daughter told me hers was here, I brought her the biggest bouquet of flowers and a card. I wanted her to remember that moment. I wanted her to feel special about the transition, I wanted her to feel celebrated.

I used to wish that I would have learned how to be strong earlier in life. I saw my mother work, I saw her cooking, some cleaning and I'm sure there were other things, but it didn't appear to be strength, it was received as survival. That is what I've learned, how to move forward from seeing what was demonstrated as survival. I never really looked at them as learning and growing tools that would make me the woman I was supposed to be. What things I could or should do and definitely what to be aware of along with what not to do. I thought maybe I wouldn't have suffered so much trying to understand what being strong meant after surviving a path of destruction towards myself and others towards me.

It wasn't until after a number of years that I began to achieve great strength. There was a time where my mother and I did not speak to one another for about two years. One day I called my mother and apologized. I apologized to her for anything that I had done or said that contributed to her hurt and our not getting along. We spoke for about two hours or so. I remember it feeling really good to speak with her and to tell her that I love her. I began to heal in the relationship with my mother because I was ready to forgive and let go of any feelings associated with the past.

Something was beginning to take shape in the relationship between my mother and myself. Full understanding wasn't revealed until later. What I did understand was, mothers are not given a parenting manual when they give birth on doing everything right. They instill and use what they know, but can they be held accountable for what they didn't know? No. Mothers use what they know, and if not taught or exposed to anything else, that's all they know.

I don't want to give the impression as though my entire childhood was absolutely horrible. The incident I shared was one from as far as I could remember which left a major impact on the lack of communication my mother and I actually had. I often felt things would have turned out differently if certain areas of my life were sown into more prolifically. However, I had to reach a point in my life where I was able to accept how everything I've experienced was a part of the process for the preparation and if something had been different, would I be in the space of peace and understanding and have the wisdom which I currently possess?

I forgive my mother for what she didn't know. I hold no ill feelings towards a path not chosen by me, but for me. The prayer for my mother is that she forgives herself for any awareness she had no knowledge of. I love you Mom.

"Children begin by loving their parents; as they grow older they judge them; sometimes they forgive them."
~Oscar Wilde

"Forgiveness is the only way to reverse the irreversible flow of history"

~ Hannah Arendt

Unchained

My Prayer for you:
I pray that you accept power for strength to forgive your mothers if you've ever felt slighted, abused or abandoned by her in any way. I pray you receive a renewal with an open mind so that you may be able to embrace the wisdom you'll gain from it. It will bring a modernization of an old history to strengthen the relationships between you and your own children.

May you be blessed to move forward in a productive life that sow's knowledge into your offspring and others who look up to you as a preparation for their offspring and generations to follow. I pray you ask for and extend forgiveness daily to increase your growth and unchain your pain.

Amen

DAY 5

Never let a relationship make you become something you're not,
because the truth is, when it's over they may never regret losing you,
but you'll always regret losing yourself.
-Sushan Sharma quo

Ending a Relationship

Then once more you shall see the distinction between the righteous and the wicked, between one who serves God and one who does not serve him.
Malachi 3:18

End: A final part of something.

Relationship: the way in which two or more concepts, objects, or people are connected, or the state of being connected.

I'm not claiming to be the most righteous woman alive, nor do I feel I am as close as I should be. I am not completely empty of all sinful behaviors, but I am a woman who is trying to get there. I know right from wrong as well as what God expects of me. I, too, fall short of those expectations. With the several types of abuse, I thought I had experienced the worst of the worst. Emotional, financial and spiritual abuse are on a whole other level. I had begun a closer relationship with God a couple of years before this last relationship and felt I was truly ready and prepared for this marriage. I was going to do it differently, I was more mature, I wasn't going to be so quick to give up and I was determined to do my part and work it out. My purpose was not revealed until I had endured this.

Personal Reflection:
We met in November of 2008. Have you ever met that one person who seemed to have come into your life at just the right time, saying the right things and so dreamy that he would just melt your heart? You'd have so many ideas and goals in common. You seemed to purely "fit together". You always want to be around each other and spend countless hours on the phone when you're not together. You say in your mind, "Yes, he's the one!" I'm sharing things about my past because the relationship was allowing me to become comfortable with him. We were on the path of a stronger commitment and over time we discussed different situations we've experienced. You want to know about him and vice versa. We're discussing one another's likes and dislikes, our families, what makes us happy, etc. etc. He shared that he had Multiple

Sclerosis and that he only smokes weed occasionally. It didn't seem to be detrimental because I know plenty of people who smoke weed; I even did a few times in high school. I've never heard of people stealing and committing other crimes to get weed. I thought it was something I didn't have an issue dealing with, I just didn't want it around me and he didn't. We had those conversations that went on for hours at a time. I would get a flutter in my heart when he called or when I knew I was going to see him. We became nonstop involved with one another. We became head over heels in love with one another and were married in July of 2009. It seemed right, safe and promising. There was a plan in place as far as what we were going to do with our lives together.

It was approximately thirty days after we were married that I came home one day and the aroma of a different scent that was not weed, filled the bathroom in my bedroom. I had never experienced anything like that odor. I learned that it was crack/cocaine. I was livid, disappointed, and sunken in a place of failure while ready to once again end a marriage. I've heard of different stories of what happens in relationships where drugs of that nature are involved. Some people lose everything behind it. They lose material items, financial stability and themselves. I remained in that marriage for several reasons, which looking at it today, made absolutely no sense. In my mind, I felt so embarrassed that I stayed to prevent exposing it. I stayed with the intention of being able to pray for a better marriage and as long as we were both going to church, God would fix it. All we were doing was going. Sometimes we'd go to church arguing, put on "the face" and we were right back, arguing when church was over and we were in the car, sometimes it began as soon as I stood up from the pew. People can be so judgmental and that's what flooded my mind. "What other people would think." Judging how I would enter relationships and not give it my all to make it work on my part, and how remaining made me feel like I was in some way defeating the patterns of my past as well as the generational patterns of most of the women in my family with failed marriages and relationships. Not paying any attention to or recognizing how the marriage was ruining any mental stability which I felt I regained after surviving my past. Had I really overcome a dysfunctional mindset or did I learn how to cope with it? Had I improved unhealthy character defects but still dealing with the same type of man? The two will never fit together. My first husband was a drug user and abusive. The last move from being with him and moved into my own apartment, he followed me and one Sunday morning he came to my apartment and stabbed in the throat twice requiring me have one hundred and two stitches to close the hole up. It was half an inch from my juggler vein. We were married for nine years. The second husband lied about how long he had been clean and stole everything he could get his hands on from the house. I was just repeating similar scenarios and each one had different forms of abuse.

What kind of husband becomes angry and calls his wife the 'B' word or an 'MF'? I had never been called either of those names in any relationship, nor had I ever been spoken to the way he spoke to me when he was angry. There were numerous apologies from him and often for the same behaviors/language. It seemed endless. He displayed very little respect for women, and over time, I learned it stemmed from his mother and how he grew up. His brother was twelve years older than him and exposed him to a very adult side of life. Multiple women, drugs, infidelity, manipulation and anger.

He knew the Bible and forgiveness was always brought up. Something he insisted I should always be willing to do because the Bible says so. We often studied together. He was an excellent teacher and he had a way of explaining things with real life situations where I could relate easier. The words of the Bible were applicable when I wasn't doing something he wanted, but totally irrelevant when he behaved in an inappropriate and disrespectful manner. No, he didn't want to hear anything in regard to his behaviors. Encouraging him to attend church regularly was not possible, especially if he smoked crack all night. Sometimes he didn't stop until the morning depending on how much he had, or how many trips he could make around the corner to get it until he ran out of money. You couldn't say anything to him, because he was just a time bomb when you did. I can't count how many things were thrown at me and against walls. So many items around the house were disappearing because he'd either break them or pawn them.

He was a functioning addict, and to look at him you'd never suspect it. I was definitely clueless. He was tall, slim, smart and extremely handsome. That appearance made it easier for him to speak negatively against me to other people and make it seem like any issue we were having was all me. He'd always claim that he wasn't a bad guy and he always does things for other people. He had dealt with a lot of women in his past, and after we were married, I found out he was maintaining inappropriate relationships. He dealt with a lot of women who also did drugs. Women who had low self-esteems and it seemed like they flocked to him because he was very nice looking and he could possibly do something for them. He knew who to deal with. Let him tell it, his wife doesn't respect him and how horrible I was to him. You know those women who feel like their opinion matters in regard to what he says he's going through and that wife just doesn't know what a great hardworking man he is. He kept the door open that allowed other women to boost his ego, and he gave the impression that he does what he wants in the marriage. There was one woman who had sent him a couple of pictures taken in a prison holding a pillow that says "I love you". One day she walked in my group. I never said anything and I treated her just as I did everyone else. My goal was to sow hope and honestly there was no issue with her. She only did what someone gave her permission to do.

I can't tell you how many times I've changed the locks on the door because he chose to stay out days at time using drugs and whatever else he was doing. I was tired of dealing with it. I was tired of him taking the television off the wall and pawning it; of his taking my jewelry until it was all gone, pawning his $2000 wedding band repeatedly that he never went to get out of the pawn shop and lost it. His obsessions were drugs, women, pornography and the pawn shop. I didn't see how I fit into any of that; perhaps I looked like a candidate to be converted into becoming an enabler, and for a while, I was. I shared some things that possibly made it seem as though I could fit, had the manipulation and control been fully successful. I started to feel I was being punished in some way for my past. I was being accused of being the reason why he keeps using drugs and keeps "female friends" on the side. He lost his driver's license many years ago and continued to drive while getting stopped by the police for speeding. He felt he was above the law and never went to court until he was incarcerated and got escorted to court. It was always everyone else's fault why he couldn't "get a break" so he could move forward. Although I had a driver's license and a job, there was no way I could transport him everywhere he had to go and be where I was supposed to. Not only did he want me to transport him, but he wanted me to wait for him while he did the job. I once took him to a customer's home and told him I couldn't stay because I had to be back at work; he said, "F your job!" His excuse for dealing with other women was for transportation because "my wife" doesn't have time. I wasn't able to see any light at the end of the tunnel. He often screamed to the top of his lungs and sometimes right in my face. He has spit in my face and threw two of my cell phones in the toilet to prevent me from being able to call the police. He tried to make me feel guilty for calling the police, that I was betraying him. He often said that was the worst thing

Unchained

I could do, as though whatever abuse that was going on in the home should have been accepted and never receive a consequence. I didn't know how to get out and stay out, when I tried, here came the manipulation again. If I meant it, I could have simply stood my ground with my decision.... or could I? Whenever we were separated, we continued to sleep with one other and before I knew it, he was moving back in.

We're in this marriage a few years and things are going back and forth with his saying he was trying to maintain sobriety. I was not a nice person to be around most of the time because I've become this angry woman who is always on the defense because I feel like I'm being judged for everything I do, picked on like a child, ridiculed, constantly being degraded as a woman, a wife and a mother. I eventually ended up feeling insecure, walking on egg shells because I'm sick and tired of arguing, the name calling, bringing up issues and incidences of my past and his telling me how I was responsible for all those things that happened in my past. Telling me that he was my only true friend and how he'd be the only one there in the end, how no one would ever love me like he does. How the friends that I had were not real friends and that my family didn't really care about me, they just use you. Many of those statements which only abusive individuals make in an effort to gain control by belittling a person and tainting their self-esteem. If I responded in a way that went against what he was saying, I was told "F" you, or "F" your mother and your family".

The smell of burning crack filled my bedroom even though he was in the bathroom with a towel on the floor at the door. There were always porn DVD's in the CD player. I remember telling him to get those drugs out of here or I was calling the police and him saying go ahead, thinking I wouldn't. I did once. When they arrived, I know they could smell it, and they didn't do a thing. That basically gave him the okay to keep doing it. Don't think I didn't get cursed out when they left. He just called one of his female friends to pick him up at the corner and was gone for a few days. He could smoke there with no problem.

Unchained

There was a time when I was feeling so depressed and it was getting worse by the day. I was absolutely miserable with this man, I loathed coming home. I didn't want to sleep in the bed with him, I didn't want him to touch me, kiss me or say anything to me. Sometimes he would come around me and if I could smell the drugs on him I would instantly change my entire demeanor. It was like a spirit had entered the atmosphere, then the anger generated in full force. He couldn't keep a job and when he had one, he smoked up his entire paycheck. He'd spend all night smoking drugs until early hours of the morning and then couldn't get up for work, but expected me to cook him breakfast before I go to work. Sometimes he'd work two days a week and had an attitude because they terminated him. One day I came home from work and all I could smell was crack burning. I was like a madwoman and I remember getting a hammer and two knives, running upstairs, banging on the bathroom door and telling him to get the hell out of my house. I felt like I was out of control of myself. Like I was trying to battle against it.

I had to do something. I couldn't focus on anything, I was late everywhere and not at all happy with my life. I went to see a therapist because I thought maybe I had ADD. I told the therapist that I needed a test or something to confirm it. After disclosing all that I had been through and was currently going through, he diagnosed me with Major Depression.

After separating for a while and him swearing things were going to be different, I told him if he stayed out just one time, that he might as well stay because the locks would be changed and there was no coming back. He said I didn't have to worry about that because it wasn't going to happen. Things seemed really good for a while.... well at least until a few weeks later when he was approved for Disability and received that back pay. He took his tool bag and walked down the street where a car was waiting for him. He said he was going to do a job and would be back in a couple of hours, it was a Thursday afternoon. The locks were changed Saturday morning. I saw him sitting on my front porch early Sunday afternoon when I was coming from church. I passed the house, called his cell phone and asked him to get off my porch. I said call whomever you were with these past couple of days and have them to pick you back up.

I just had to build and keep enough strength and determination to stand my ground and carry out what I said. I had had enough. I needed some peace. Something I was without for a very long time. I was lost with where I was going to begin to piece my life back together. My faith was long and strong and I asked God to help me. I found myself in a state of humbled repentance to God because I had chosen wrong too many times, and this final time, I could not find the strength nor the sanity to be open enough to remain in this marriage any longer hoping for the possibility of a healthy and functional shift. I felt as though I was losing myself by staying in it, but at the same time being strengthened at the thought of leaving. The relationship ended in August of 2014.

My prayer for you:
I pray you receive the healing that is most necessary to move forward from any situation you are in or have been in which is or has caused brokenness within your life. I send up prayers of strength and an

openness for understanding with your name on it which not only allows you to receive peace towards your next move, but also the revelation from the lesson you needed to embrace from it to be realigned towards God's purpose for your life. Safe Blessings to the broken-hearted. Be empowered to move out of your way and let God lead you.

Amen

DAY 6

A memorable moment about my Family

Life goes by in the blink of an eye. So be sure to appreciate the many moments with family and friends that make your life complete.
~Author Unknown

Memorable: Worth remembering or easily remembered, especially because of being special or unusual.

Family: A group of people regarded as deriving from a common stock.

There are always those precious moments about our lives that are truly worth remembering. Events we hold close to our heart because they make us feel so good on the inside. As life goes on and we encounter new experiences, they may have a tendency to surpass the feelings of a past event; yet and still, they become a most memorable moment.

Personal Reflection:
The most memorable moment about my family that makes my heart flutter at the thought, is when my daughter graduated high school. Although many parents can attest to the same feeling of being proud when their children graduate high school, my personal experience was a bit different than the traditional celebration. My daughter dropped out of high school when she was sixteen years old. She was defiant, rebellious, had a low self-esteem and just wanted to do what she wanted to do and when she got good and ready. We were two balls of dysfunction clashing into one another and not accomplishing anything productive or conducive to a normal mother-daughter relationship/bond. We weren't normal as society would deem us. We both had experiences in our lives that greatly affected a healthy and functional journey in life, and my lack of effective parenting abilities were a major contributor. For a minute, I felt some type of way about actually writing, ***"My lack of effective parenting abilities".*** I had to come to the understanding that if I try and hide things within myself that are the truth; as embarrassing and incompetent as it once made me

Unchained

feel, acceptance and growth would have never found me. I had to receive there was a deficit on my part. I had to accept where it came from and correct it. I had to commit to forgiving myself and moving forward. Not being able to admit that would have created a delay in my process. I don't want to prevent the opportunity for someone else who may be struggling with a similar situation to miss the revelation of being able to move forward. Although my daughter and I didn't see eye-to-eye on too many things in her teen years and well into her early twenties, her incarceration eventually turned things around for the both of us. We were both incarcerated at the same time, I just wasn't behind the same kind of bars she was.

My daughter began taking General Equivalency Diploma classes while she was incarcerated, and had high expectations when she was released to finish what she'd started. She began attending a program at the Peninsula Work Link and completed various assessments. She found out she was able to take classes to receive her high school diploma. We all have areas in our lives that we may struggle in, and many people have a different way of learning in those areas. When she began to verbalize the struggles she was experiencing, I remember encouraging her to use whatever services they offer to make sure she understood what she was doing. People can't read our minds to know when and what we need help with. There are many resources available, but you have to tell someone when and with what you need help. If they don't know, they can usually refer you to someone or someplace that can help you.

Her persistence and determination was so amazing to me. She never allowed anything nor anyone to deter her from what she was doing. She even passed on a few dinner dates with me when I was off from work. She said, "Sorry mom, I can't, I have to go to tutoring tonight!" Those moments stick in my head because she doesn't usually pass up a free meal, especially with her mom.

When she completed the program and passed all of the requirements, it was just a matter of time before the actual graduation ceremony date. When I saw her in her white cap and gown..........my heart was full!! I had so many emotions running through me and I began to get overwhelmed with joy. I did really well with holding back the tears that wanted to burst out from excitement for her, but that went out the window when she walked across that stage. To see my baby walking the stage to receive her High School Diploma was a feeling that consumed my entire body. I could not have been more proud of her accomplishment. I wanted that for her so much. I shared with her how excited I was for her to experience walking the stage as a celebration for all that she had accomplished and it will be a memory she'll never forget. The journey she had to travel to get there made it an even more celebratory event.

My prayer for you:
Never stop dreaming. Dreams can become a reality in your life. Holding onto your past, things you feel less confident about, lack of knowledge or inadequacies have a power that can cripple us. I pray that you open yourselves to receive the understanding that all of what you have experienced, both good and unpleasant were needed to become all of who you are destined to be. Ask yourself what value it has to you by holding onto those

circumstances and continuously dragging them, not only throughout your life, but the life of others who enter your life. These circumstances are thorns in your flesh. You will always remember how painful they were, but at the same time, they serve a useful purpose. They are not placed there for you to become destructive of yourselves, but to ignite the power within you to serve in a capacity in which only you were purposed for. They contribute to your divine purpose with humility. The thorns are only painful if your sole focus is the pain that put them there. Reformulate your perception of the thorn and use it for your good and the good of others. Grant yourself the permission to heal. God is right there to move you through the rest. If you say "YES", He hears you and the transformation begins.

Amen

DAY 7

"Things turn out the best
for the people who make the best
of the way things turn out."
-John Wooden

What Family Means to Me

Family is like branches on a tree, our lives may grow in different directions but our roots will stay as one.
~Unknown Author

Family: A basic social unit consisting of parents and their children, considered as a group, whether dwelling together or not

Depending on how and where you were raised, most of us grew up believing that the "family" was a group of relatives that we'd age with. We'd have holiday get-togethers and other gatherings. We'd often look forward to long distance relatives who were planning to come and we'd all have such a wonderful time being together. The aroma from all the food the older relatives prepared flooded the house and as the children played outside, we couldn't wait until it was time to eat. There was always that one aunt, uncle or cousin who'd have entirely too much to drink and begin to act a fool. We'd all whisper to one another how they always act like that whenever they come around, yet; we couldn't wait for them to get here, every year. We simply enjoyed being in the presence of one another. We'd laugh uncontrollably at the silliest of things, then talk about its memory for the longest of times.

Personal Reflection:
Being in the presence of one another was what I most looked forward to. No matter what was happening behind closed doors, our focus was never on those situations. Many years lapsed, well after we were all grown before I would receive that the majority of us were dysfunctional to some degree. We were mentally unhealthy. I don't want to point blame at any one specific individual or even a select few, it's just an observation of how the mindset is developed by what we are and aren't exposed to as children and how it shapes the acceptance or rejection of the choices we make as we grow through our lives.

We used to have these really big cookouts on the 4th of July at our home in Bay Shore, New York where my brother and I grew up. We had gotten a pool and

I remember it being so much fun because we were all together. I don't even know why we stopped having them, but one year it all stopped. At some point we all began growing apart.

Three years after I moved to Virginia I bought a home. Several years afterwards I decided to begin having an annual 4th of July cookout. My family was still somewhat distant and the only time we came together was to attend a funeral, a wedding or a crisis of some sort. The intention of the cookout was to bring my family together as we used to long ago. Several family members had relocated to VA and we were all a little closer. Although some were still in New York, a couple would still come.

We even had a lady's night the day before so that we could prep most of the food, but I think we consumed cocktails and laughed more than anything else. Everyone would contribute by bringing something and we'd have the best time, well for a while anyway. It was only a matter of time before those deep-rooted and unresolved family issues began to surface and the judging of one another eroded the good times we used to have. This one got on that one's nerve, she said this, she acts like that, etc. etc. The occasion eventually lost its focus and purpose and it started to become more of a mental struggle trying to hold it together. We lack the necessary tools for healthy development and very few of us managed to overcome the severity of the impact it had. It became a prevalent but silent deterioration of our family connection.

It's been a few years since we've had the cookout, and recently my brother suggested we try it again. My brother and I began having Sunday Family Dinners for the past few months, and that's been going really fantastic, so......we'll see. I'm considering it. Family love and togetherness is very important and healthy for me.

My prayer for you:
I pray you receive understanding of not being expected to save the members of your family from the issues within the family. Understanding that each person must deal with their own personal feelings related to those issues which keep you in detachment. I pray you receive the ability to accept

and restore your portion that contributes to any dysfunction in your family circle. Not only do I pray this for you, but I pray the same for each member of your family. May all who have been affected by a "secret" never told, but demonstrated in negative and consequential behaviors be released from it by voicing it and enter the road of forgiveness to enable peace and solidarity to move you all forward in order to embrace and celebrate the true meaning of what family stands for. I pray you accept purification of deadened roots be cleansed and shaken together for new life and acted upon the fruit of the Holy Spirit.

Amen

DAY 8

"The greatest glory in living lies not in never failing,
but in rising every time we fail."
~Nelson Mandela

A Real Life Super Woman

And we know that all things work together for good to those who love God, to those who are the called according to His purpose.
Romans 8:28

Real: Actually existing as a thing or occurring in fact; not imagined or supposed.

Super Woman: A woman with exceptional strength or ability, especially one who successfully manages a home, brings up children, and has a full-time job.

We may feel as though we don't come close to being a super woman if one or more of the above isn't included in our daily lives. We may be in situations which limit us from fulfilling those that we feel we do not possess. Through the spirit of Gods power, we are able to achieve all of them. We don't always know how to deviate from the roads we journey which cause us to not walk in the direction of our purpose in life, situations which cause us to feel degraded or powerless, and even circumstances that limit our believing that we are important to this world and the one in the hereafter. I believe we all have the capability and the only thing that separates us is the way we think of ourselves and why we remain in existence. When we overcome obstacles, we're positioned to bare good fruit and present lasting life lessons on others as we continue to move forward in our own lives.

Personal Reflection:
I've never heard of a super woman when I was growing up. To me, they were cartoons or fictional characters on television. There were no inspirational women in my family and I don't recall knowing any that I was ever inspired by during my childhood. I don't really recall my being exposed to any fascinating women that left a lasting impression on me. I didn't know what an inspirational woman was.

I've completed one semester of college and never went back to complete a degree because I was working two jobs with a young child and couldn't grasped how to manage doing it all. I had a car payment and a mortgage with all the expenses that come with owning a home. I never felt like I had really accomplished anything major other than, staying employed, being a homeowner and having multiple unhealthy relationships. My brother and I grew up in a home and my mother worked, I grew up knowing how to do those two things. I had no professional focus in life and wasn't particularly sure what it was I was supposed to be doing in this life. I lacked insight of where I actually wanted to be in five or ten years, actually from year to year. I didn't have a vision of what I wanted to be when I grew up like some other children had. I'm not sure as to why I didn't dream of being someone or something specific, it just wasn't really in me to see ahead that far in advance. Right here, right now is what I knew. I do remember writing poetry as a teen but never pursued a career direction with it. It was just something I used to do. As I reflect back to those days, I was basically writing the feelings I had during those times. I released what was and was not within me onto paper. I wrote about love, being beautiful and lovely things that were beautiful.

What is amazing to me, when I facilitate WE1A groups in correctional facilities, I promote, encourage and empower women to embrace their inner beauty and loving themselves. My passion for love and inner beauty was within me as a young girl. The seed was already there, the thorns of my life would bring it to fruition. Isn't that something worthy of a praise? Who knew......but God. I speak with these women and remind them of how beautiful they are, on the inside. How powerful God created us and because of our unfortunate experiences in life, we don't always see it or believe it. We more often than not have a tendency to only see what is tangibly in front of us and the possibility of there being anything else is oblivious.

I was often a humorist during childhood. I didn't really take things too seriously and laughter was my way of not truly feeling and dealing with the issues within me head on. As I grew older, I maintained a good sense of humor and it definitely helped to prevent becoming consumed with what was going on within and around me as I learned how to face my issues and put more productive measures to use. I just kept going and if I tripped and fell, it was only a matter of time before I got right back up. Evidently I hadn't fallen hard enough because once I got up I was basically doing things the same way once the pain subsided. Sometimes we have to fall several times before we're like, "wait a minute, this is really beginning to be painful and I need to make a change!" Even after that light bulb in our brain shines at its brightest, some of us still go through similar situations again. With our eternal epiphany, we don't automatically develop a mindset of how to actually do something differently? We don't know how we are supposed to execute this required change and we end up deepening those same wounds that can result in years of hurt. We made it harder to get to because of its depth. Not that we wanted it to, but it was how things went.

My faith in God grew closer and the relationship showed me who and whose I was. I was enlightened with understanding of why I endured all that I had and why I triumphed over the obstacles, bumps, holes, bruises, pain and abuse. I was shown how my way of learning was through life itself. I often became overwhelmed, in a good way, at the thought of God choosing me for this purpose. I'm not a doctor, psychologist, professor or even a pastor, I'm me. Just as He created me to be. I came to the understanding that my entire life was a preparation for the plan He purposed for me. I had to not only accept it, but be obedient in it for me to move towards the direction He saw I would be most effective. It would allow me to utilize my personal experiences and enable me to witness who God is my life. God will use you! Under any circumstances and from any background. Sometimes people feel that they've figured it all out on their own. However, when God positions you for an assignment, walking any other path than His, prevents the intended fulfillment He planned not just for you but for His divine glory. Seeking and asking God to order your steps shall keep you in perfect peace.

In actuality, all women can be considered a "super woman". It takes the birth of our own belief in ourselves with the knowledge and activation of the power already built within us. That internal power ignites the drive we need to move forward. We'll always have multiple responsibilities that have a necessary simultaneous completion at one point or another in our lives. We should never play small the capabilities we have inside. Although we may not be as successful as we'd like to be in everything we do, don't knock yourself for at least making an attempt. We have to keep trying and what's supposed to work out will. A super woman doesn't give up. She keeps going. She continues her journey in her faith and strives to be all she can possibly be.

My prayer for you:
I pray when your purpose in life presents itself that you grasp it and not turn away with uncertainty or apprehension if it does not appear as the plan "you" had prepared for. What you may have had planned for your life can be totally contrary to the divine purpose specifically planned only for you as evidenced during your years of preparation through your experiences. I pray you embrace the "super woman" within you while revealing and empowering the greatest depth of your understanding and acceptance to enable you to walk in peace, prosperity and amazement of how all you've

successfully endured was a plan to get you to your divine call.

Amen

DAY 9

Picking up The Pieces

For I know the thoughts that I think toward you, says the Lord, thoughts of peace and not of evil, to give you a future and a hope.
Jeremiah 29:11

Picking up: To gather in

Pieces: A portion of an object or of material, produced by cutting, tearing, or breaking the whole.

How do we arrive to the realization that we need to begin picking up the pieces? At what point in our lives does it surface? How is it pushed to the forefront of our mindset? After all of the disappointment and uncertainty brought on by various occurrences, can we actually push through all of those damaging entities which have created our brokenness? Most of us can't actually vision ourselves moving through the storm. We begin suppressing the feelings associated with our pain inviting numerous unhealthy habits and behaviors which then adds to an already toxic lifestyle. We become complacent in them because in our minds, as long as we do not feel any imminent pain "we're good". We begin believing if we can continue to suppress these feelings they will not surface. "If I don't think about it and do not allow others to know about it, I'm safe; no one gets in and "my stuff" doesn't get out". We've created our normalcy. We've adapted to hiding within ourselves believing there's an expectation of successfully going around, over and under the storm and not actually realizing going through those storms will make us successors of freedom within.

Personal Reflection:
It was a very long time before I actually began to understand how being exposed on a daily basis to an unhealthy, abusive, manipulative, controlling and dysfunctional environment was affecting me. I feel like it molded and shaped me to receive it from other relationships; those similar traits and behaviors which was my normalcy.

I was tired of feeling like I was unworthy, under-loved, unappreciated and without direction towards a meaningful and fulfilling life. When there is a plan already destined for your life, who better to consult and connect with other than that power in you which is greater than you. I began to fellowship regularly again and hear the word of God; not only hearing but feeling. I was finding things to keep myself inspired, and I communicated more with God in order to hear what it was that I was supposed to be doing with my life. All of it didn't come at once and trust me, it wasn't easy. One day at a time with one breath at a time. My determination to become someone with substance came alive when I began sowing into others. As I put together my curriculum for the women in the jails, the topics that came to mind appeared to also be topics I myself needed. I didn't realize it until I started to write this book. It all worked together. I was aware that I wasn't totally healed from my past, but I felt the healing coming about as I spoke those topics into the women in the group. As I shared of myself the things I had experienced, it became a group of healing. I shared real life examples of what I experienced and their attentiveness to what I was sharing was incredible to me. I didn't deliberately set it up like that, it was destined to happen in a manner where I would heal.

Unchained

It was destiny. The part I played, obedience. Obedience to what I felt and believed in my heart I was being lead to do. I was already prepared, I had lived it, and I survived it. I only needed to creatively figure out how to put it on paper and execute it while keeping God in the center of all of it in order for it to happen the way it's supposed to. I distinctively recall the very first day I covered how to recognize abusive relationships. As I listed those traits of an abusive person, I became so convicted. Here I am explaining the signs of an abusive person, and I was in one. Again, I was married to one. I was feeling that conviction on a daily basis. Destiny prevailed yet again, at a time when I was able to become detached from my abusive relationship. I felt like I was able to finally breathe air in which I was supposed to. This was it. I had to position myself to move forward and take all of what I've learned from the lesson. I became more focused on what I was doing and began to move into other correctional facilities where I could begin my women empowerment group. I was learning and healing as I was teaching and sowing.

My broken pieces had been bonded together to create a wholeness within me. When I allowed myself permission to be free from those entities that kept me complacent in not living the way in which I should have been. Being imprisoned behind bars isn't the only way a person can be incarcerated. We can maintain our own individualized incarceration within our minds. Not having the knowledge to release matters create paralyzing effects on our capabilities to move forward. We must decide within ourselves that we are tired of unhealthy mindsets which have negative and unproductive results in our lives. We have to choose. No one can make the decision for us.

My prayer for you:
I pray you surrender to the healing and mending of the broken pieces within you. I pray you receive it in a mighty way. May all you've endured remain a memory as your new strength overtakes you and keeps you connected to that power that motivates you each day as your journey reveals it was all a part of the preparation.

Amen

DAY 10

The Giver Syndrome

Give, and it will be given to you. A good measure, pressed down, shaken together and running over, will be poured into your lap. For with the measure you use, it will be measured to you.
Luke 6:38

Giver: A person who gives something

Syndrome: A characteristic combination of opinions, emotions, or behavior.

If you are a person who has a giving nature and you suddenly come faced with an obstruction in your life, you can at times feel you no longer have any more of yourself to give. The giving spirit is still within you and it will always be there, it may temporarily lie dormant during a storm simply because you may not have mastered that specific process yet.

Personal Reflection:
We give because it's just in us to do so. We've grown into being givers because it makes us feel good to allow others to feel good. We sometimes get taken

advantage of. People don't always appreciate a person who gives from the heart and when an unjustified or abusive behavior occurs as an eventual response, we can find ourselves at a momentary standstill because we don't always know what to do next. We can find ourselves questioning whether we did something erroneous as though our intent wasn't genuine. Although the enemy can come with considerable trickery, we always have the choice to make that trickery a non-entity in who and how we choose to live day to day.

I was once involved with a man who I allowed to bring out the very worst version of myself. I was in a relationship that caused me to not feel as though I was elevating as a woman or wife, but falling into a position to lose my sense of self.... or did I actually know who I was in order to receive that I was losing myself? If you don't know where you are or where you're supposed to be, how do you know you're not already there? You do know something doesn't feel quite the way it should. I wasn't receiving the joy of giving the way I should have been. The more I gave, the more he took, the more he expected, the less he

Unchained

gave, and the worse I felt as though I weren't giving enough.

I'm in no way suggesting giving is a bad thing. This is true for both male and female relationships. We can sometimes choose the wrong individual to give to and we can give too much, too frequently and definitely too soon. Although our intention isn't to only to receive when you're in a relationship, the natural expectation is for it to be reciprocated as the two of you move forward in that relationship. As we grow together, a healthy relationship elevates us into the best versions of ourselves. I believe when we are not mentally and or emotionally vigorous in our thinking, we can take on numerous thought processes regarding how we choose to receive the lack of reciprocation of our involvement with others. When we have not accepted a friendship for the right reasons, it will surely prove itself and at times, not so pleasantly. People who are only "takers" are out for what they can get from whoever will give it, which is often a sign of a destructive person with no intention to build. There must be a conscious understanding and acceptance towards exactly who we're dealing with and the lesson to be learned as to why a person has entered our lives.

My prayer for you:
May God continue to bless all of who you are, what you experience and where you are going in your giving. May the spirit that dwells in you come alive in a mighty way and shine its brightest in your life as you journey to your intended purpose destined only for you.

DAY 11

A Relationship with Myself

We all come into and go out of this world in the same way. The destination is the same. The difference is the Journey. Some enjoy it, some don't!
Author Unknown

Relationship: the way in which two or more concepts, objects, or people are connected, or the state of being connected.

Myself: I or me personally.

Some women can go most of their lives without totally fulfilling relationships. Unfortunately, this is not that, "I found love after abuse" book. Not the kind of love with a mate, but the love of myself and the acceptance of the assignment for helping others to do the same. Can I first learn to have a loving relationship with myself to prevent the continued attraction of "Mr. Wrong" or unhealthy relationships with female friends? I've hardly ever been "single", and for the past three years, not only have I been single but I've been positioned to have the greatest opportunity to love on me and consciously healthy relationships with others. To have accepted the totally fulfilling assignment of sowing into others using what I've experienced in my life has given me more self-satisfaction than I could have ever imagined to receive. Anything after this is just a bonus for my obedience.

Personal Reflection:
We seldom do self-evaluations while we're in a relationship. It more often than not, comes after the relationship has gone sour and we're trying to recover from the heartbreak, disappointment and even the bitterness. As I'm writing this book, it is allowing me to put my dissected life on paper while embracing the revelation of how I actually got to this point as the successor of what I've experienced. As women, we don't always take care of ourselves first in order to be available for others when they need us. We're nurturers by nature and we often get what's left, if there is anything after we've given it all away with no replenishment. I've spent countless years giving of myself not realizing that no one was taking care of me, not even me.

Unchained

I have received how to learn as I empower others. I handle my relationships with others better, and I often evaluate whether my relationships are two-sided or just my putting forth an effort and the other party not cherishing or nurturing the relationship in a manner that is healthy for me. People can mentally drain all of you and not be positioned to sow back into you. Some people will at times want you to always be a listening ear and they may not want your advice every time, which is okay, but at what point are you able to count on that same person/people to be available or even interested in what you may need from the relationship? A relationship between two people can become that "giver" syndrome where you're always giving but not receiving. Trust me, some people are fine with that. They are complacent with the thought of, "That's my girl, she doesn't mind" or "Oh, she's my friend, she'll always listen to me." Is that always enough, or do we simply allow someone to drain us until there's nothing left. I had to release several relationships because not only were they not healthy, but they weren't allowing me feel like I was growing as a person. For a very long time I didn't even know what a true relationship was? What I had known of a relationship wasn't the healthiest experience growing up. No one ever suggested getting out of an abusive situation. You're married, that's your husband, you stick it out.... even if it kills you? Was I ever exposed to what a genuinely healthy relationship looked like, or were they simply visions of arrangements for convenience? I thought I knew what true love was between two people when I met my 1st husband. Maybe it was due to his showing me a love which was more so safety and protection. Could it have been that he rescued me from an abusive childhood, which actually ended up as my being transferred into another abusive relationship on a different level that ultimately almost cost me my life.

I had to find my way. I had to make a decision with a commitment to take what I had been through and use it to the best of my ability. Although there was a lot of pain along my journey of who I am today, the old saying of what doesn't kill us makes us stronger held true for me. I'm still here and doing a work prepared just for me. Acknowledging who and who's I am spiritually, gave me the inner peace I've been without, or if in fact it was already there, I didn't know how to ignite it.

The types of relationships I hold with others is an extension of who I am and contribute a wholeness within me. I surround myself with people I have an appreciation for because I'm able to learn so much from them. Their spirit is a contributor to the balance within me. Some of them are also survivors of situations that had broken them down, but they've moved forward and their strength is admirable to me.

My prayer for you:
In all you do, I pray you receive and use the lessons learned for your own divine preparation. I pray for strength and comfort during those times when you feel you just can't go on, you can and you will if you faint not. Situations that are out of our control are always within God's reach. I pray you use the spirit of God to enjoy the loving relationship with yourself which is much needed for a healthy balance in your life. May you be filled with all the desires of your heart that God has just for you to live your best life.... NOW.

Amen

Unchained

DAY 12

Experience is not what happens to you;
it is what you do with what happens to you.
~Aldous Huxley

Cast Out Unbelief

Why don't you start believing that no matter what you have or haven't done, that your best days are still out in front of you.
~Joel Osteen

Cast out: To drive out

Unbelief: The refusal or reluctance to believe

No one can force you to believe in yourself or what you're capable of accomplishing in your life. If you're at a point where you can't quite see that far yet, start with today. It has to come from within you. Although you may be receptive to suggestions on how you can begin this process and ways to get to the place you intend, you must begin the process to cast out unbelief. You must be the one to accept, believe and move in the possibility of it actually coming to fruition.

Personal Reflection:

There will always be people who don't believe previously incarcerated individuals deserve another opportunity to redeem themselves and live productive lives. The odds can be against you in so many different areas of your journey to sustainability. As I continue to facilitate weekly empowerment groups in correctional facilities with the women, it enables me the opportunity to get to know a lot about them; their histories, their traumas and the goals they once had for their lives. I don't ask their charges for a couple of reasons. I never want them to feel as though I'm judging in any way, nor do I want them to feel as if I'm speaking directly to their specific situation. I never want there to be any resistance in sharing while participating in the groups and I feel if they think the group positions them for any degradation they'll become reluctant to attend. I speak to them in a group with no partiality. I sow hope into each and every one of them. I embrace their struggles. We are all different shapes, sizes, shades, ages and have different beliefs, but the one thing we do have in common, we're all women. We're women who more often than not react according to our emotions. We

Unchained

make decisions based on what was and was not taught and learned during our upbringing. Those decisions often have results which are consequential. These women are not bad people, they've made some bad decisions and a few more than others. Unfortunately, many people have a preference to not work with this population. I'm not justifying or making excuses for a person who breaks the law, I understand there is a consequence in doing so. Jails are not rehabilitation though; jails cannot address the needs of each individual serving time. They are like holding cages that are sometimes overcrowded. They do offer a couple of groups that the inmates can attend, but it is up to compassionate volunteers with an inner desire to utilize their gifts and fruit to come inside correctional facilities and work with them. WE1A, INC. provides a platform for incarcerated women to put specific issues on the table and talk about them. There are no professional psychoanalytical assessments taking place. It's a strictly informal yet effective approach to some of the issues that affect women. We have "girl talk" as we create a "Sistahood" between the participants. They cry together, embrace one another and laugh together. By completing their written assignments, they sow into one another as they liberate each other to do the same. There are more women who refuse to take the group than those who choose to attend. When other women hear what is required for participation, they're just not ready. They have no openness towards addressing where their hurt and anger stem from. Some are also emotionally threatened by other women discussing what they've been through. It does happen sometimes. I can't fault them in any way, it can be extremely overwhelming and the actuality of addressing those feelings can be too much to bear for other women to go back and break confidentiality. Sadly, some women never get to the point of addressing enough or any of those deep-rooted issues which is sure to begin a healing force that's required to successfully move forward from their pasts and towards productive lives. Some broken women can become so complacent in that downward spiral because it's familiar, they know how to do that. Doing anything outside of that causes a discomfort with a challenge they're just not emotionally or mentally ready to take on. The "start" on their journey to internal freedom

Unchained

cannot take a mental shape of an actual possibility when there's no openness.

Mentally casting out unbelief is a process that must take place. When we activate that mustard seed size of faith, it can be done. We have to want it as well as believe it can be done. We must open our deepest desire for change and go for it. We're slow to realize there's nothing to lose, but actually everything to gain. Positioning ourselves to unchain generational patterns by dislodging that link which keeps us connected to remaining in the unbelief stunts our growth.

For anyone who did not have an advantage of having the following sown into you at an early stage of life, allow me to sow into you myself, right here and right now:

- You are powerful
- You are beautiful
- You are an amazing soul
- You have purpose
- You can do this
- You are enough
- I love you

We must always continue building up our inner selves. We will fall short in some area or another, everyone does. Even the best of the very best fall a little short somewhere. No one is perfect and no matter what the upbringing, education, financial status, titles, accomplishments, etc. etc., no one makes everything about themselves or life itself perfect. We can always learn. We cease our learning when we deny an opportunity. We cannot ever learn enough about everything. We should always have a willingness to receive a little more where and when possible. We should always use those areas which aren't broken within us to make us stronger in order to heal the areas that are broken.

For most of the women who do attend and complete all of the assignments, they actually gain an understanding of where things began to go left. They work through those issues while being supported within the group. Our statistics show that over our three-year period approximately 1900 women have attended the empowerment group in the various facilities. For the women who have attended the group and have been released, the recidivism rate of those women has been lowered, some were transferred to prisons or a rehabilitation facility such a drug program or another therapeutic program, but when and if they return, most sign back up for the group. A couple of women said thcy believe they didn't take it as serious as they should have and how easy it was to go right back with the previous crowd thinking they were strong enough to fight the temptation. If you leave with the same unaddressed issues as you came in with, you're going to return with those same unaddressed issues, and sometimes more intensified. It will remain a cycle in your life and you will become the example gencrations after you follow suit. Children exemplify the same ethical and moral standards you have or the lack thereof, how you make decisions and your repetitive incarceration, that's what they'll know, what you do.

You can't expect that serving time while not doing anything productive, just playing spades, receiving and/or trading commissary, making phone calls, or trying to be the #1 drama queen of the pod, will improve the issues that caused the bad decision making which has brought or keeps bringing you to jail. You pass time, but you must position yourself to cast out those things that are not going to move you forward. You must make an effort to believe in yourself. You cannot allow the disbelief to take precedence over the good in you, it's too toxic. You have to make your well-being a priority. Your purpose is awaiting your arrival from all of what you've been through as you make the decision to conquer them.

My prayer for you:
I pray that you receive how understanding is already within us and deny choosing to not receive it. We sometimes can't imagine peace within us due to the lack of self-confidence that we can conquer the pain. I pray it explodes in the pit of your being to enable a fire in you for the life destined for you.   *Amen*

DAY 13

"It is always important to know when something has reached its end. Closing circles, shutting doors, finishing chapters, it doesn't matter what we call it; what matters is to leave in the past those moments in life that are over."
~Paulo Coelho, The Zahir

Moving Forward

"Don't copy the behavior and customs of this world, but let God transform you into a new person by changing the way you think. Then you will learn to know God's will for you, which is good and pleasing and perfect."
Romans 12:2

Moving: Producing or transferring motion or action

Forward: Of, relating to, or getting ready for the future

Moving forward can be such a difficult task to begin. We're sometimes slow to even position ourselves in the direction we need to be. We are all faced with challenges at one point or another which can keep us anchored in fear and cause us to not believe that we can overcome whatever obstacles we stumble upon. We cannot always complete every task on our own, nor do we have to. Discover your internal source of strength which will not only point you in the destined direction, but will also carry you through.

Personal Reflection:
Moving forward is a mindset. Our environment, the individuals we choose to keep the company of and a tainted or lack of positive self-esteem can all affect our ability to make the decision to move forward. When we are experiencing a series of events that do not seem to be moving in the intended direction, we can become so discouraged and even lose any drive we may have had to keep pushing forward. As I strive to build my Supportive Living environment for women being released from jails & prisons, I come across people who are not only non-supportive, but their attempt to be discouraging is totally abysmal. Some people know they can be entirely too opinionated, especially when you haven't asked. When we are purposed for an assignment, we may at times require a reminder of why we began the specific path you're on in the first place. It is necessary to pray away any negativity that the enemy attempts to use others to sow into you. Although my Women's Empowerment program is not labeled or categorized "spiritual" or "religious", God is in the center of my organization, I

keep Him there. The spirit is in me and His spirit is what keeps me motivated. He gave me this assignment and facilitating the empowerment groups fulfills me. I sow hope into my ladies, and they definitely sow into me.

Some of the women come into the group not always knowing what to expect. They have no idea about what takes place in the group. My groups aren't scripted, they're real. Real life topics and real life experiences to go with them. We create a toolbox of affirmations to enable the women to fill themselves with positive expressions and we suggest they read them daily, not just once a day, but as often as possible throughout the day. My life is full of feedback and there aren't too many situations I haven't experienced, there are some, but not many. I've had my share of dysfunction as a child as well as into my adult years. My responses to the women are genuine and sincere. I use the sexual abuse of a step-father, failed relationships, the near death experience from being stabbed in the throat by my first husband, the disconnected relationship with my mother, the nonexistence of my father and the anger and bad decision making which stemmed from all of it.

I believe my triumphs over all I've endured was destined in order for me to receive a well-rounded preparation to carry out my very special assignment designed and chosen for me. We are all chosen for specific assignments in this life. We do not have to measure up to what others are doing or plan to do. The only way I would have come to this understanding was through a relationship with the God I serve. I could not have learned what has occurred in my past and present any other way than to have gone through it and conquered the possibilities of what the end result could have been had there not been a deepened desire to move forward which only I could have pulled up at the root. I chose to no longer be depressed, to not be a victim, to not blame others and to not succumb to the criticisms of others and all of their opinions which bear no weight or influence on my journey. I use my life to strengthen the brokenness in the lives of the women who take the group. My life is not all of where it should be, yet. I continue to strive to be better than the day before and to be more effective in any way I can. The gratefulness that floods my being on a daily basis reignites my drive to keep pushing and not stop or waver. I use my present life to encourage them. I bring love and hope to support the women who have a desire and a willingness to do something different. To encourage how they have nothing to lose other than their old way of thinking and their non-productive way of living.

I am not the only one to be healed of such circumstances. Anyone experiencing any form of brokenness can be healed and move forward, should we decide to choose the path which needs to be taken. We're not always aware or motivated to take that first step. We can spend an endless amount of time trying to figure out the entire layout of how we think we should begin, but the most crucial step is to make the decision to do so. You can do it, and you don't have to do it alone. There is power in you which only requires being activated. We play ourselves short not realizing how much inner strength we already have.

Those you least expect to turn their backs on you, will be the first to deny and or reject those efforts. They will continuously judge you for various reasons. If you are a person who has an unpleasant history with people, especially family or close friends who have given you chance after chance, and sometimes another chance after that, their belief in you ever getting your life together could have grown very slim. They may not know what to believe as far as you're concerned. They may have heard you claim the last time was the last time.

Moving forward does not mean you automatically receive a pardon with loved one's you've affected with your previous behaviors and mistrust. Call it what it is, and don't deny the part you've played in contributing to the way some of them feel towards you. There is a judge at the end and it will not be your loved ones or friends who will stand before the ultimate judge with you. It will be just you, and you do not have time to people please. Your decision to move forward and walk out on that false version of you that kept you anchored in not carrying out the purpose planned for you must and will be your focus.

It's in that moment of acceptance where you will begin to embrace why you have been given grace and mercy all this time, even when some of your previous acquaintances have left this world. In your darkest hour, He kept you, why? Your purpose is why and it cannot be fulfilled if you're not here to do it. We are not in existence to suffer, live in fear or amount to nothing. Even when you feel you're down to nothing, God is always up to something. Be bold in your walk.

My prayer for you:

I pray for your ability to release the peace which currently lies within you however; is bound with internal unaddressed matters. I pray the arrival of the major shift that will take place in your life finds you fully undefended and prepared to move forward. Prayers for you to receive how very special you are and the importance of the position you're already purposed for, once you make the decision to accept it. Prayers that any attempted attacks of the enemy be rebuked. Prayers that you never cease or diminish your self-confidence in spite of those who reject you and your sincere efforts to begin again by walking in the transformed newness within you.

Amen

Unchained

Unchained

DAY 14

Having a low opinion of yourself is not "modesty".
It's self-destruction.
Holding your uniqueness in high regard is not
"egotism".
It's a necessary precondition to happiness and
success.
~Bobbe Sommer

My Self-Esteem Made Me Do It

For God has not given us a spirit of fear, but of power
and of love and of a sound mind.
2 Timothy 1:7

Self-Esteem: A feeling of satisfaction that someone
has in themselves and or their own abilities.

The level of your self-esteem is the determining factor
which allows how you make decisions in and for your
life. The way you feel about yourself produces the
confidence towards a path of success or it can create
destructiveness. How self-esteem is derived is
majorly dependent upon the way in which you've
learned or observed how to build it within.

Personal Reflection:
Growing up, the importance of developing a high self-
esteem was not sown into me. As a result, trial and
error became my teachers. Although my past wasn't

as pleasant as I may have preferred it to be, I don't live in regret because of it. I'm not necessarily proud of every decision I've made throughout my life but the path I've ended up on is one that was divinely prepared for me, just as one is awaiting you.

Some of the choices which I have made in my life brought about many painful and disappointing results and "going through to get to" was a solid factor in the high self-esteem I've developed within myself over the past few years. When there is an understanding and acceptance of what you do and don't know, along with a desire to be and do better, changes can occur. There's a powerful force within all of us that becomes awakened when the desire to do better becomes stronger than the complacency in doing nothing. I became disturbed in living without any substantial meaning to my life. There was something special in me and I didn't know how to bring it out.

Those thoughts of doing something great with my life came long ago. However, the lack of a high self-esteem or the belief that I could possibly do something outside of my every day or even something extraordinary seemed unattainable. In order for me to receive how all of what I've gone through in my life was a part of the plan to be used to carry out my purpose, I had to self-evaluate my life and begin making some decisions. I needed the inner strength to think outside the box because maintaining my current thinking within the same scope would not present different results. How would I have reached where I am today if there was not something beforehand awaiting the spark? The answer was within me through the power greater than me and I had to choose to be obedient to the feelings which seemed like they were trying to burst out.

If you choose to only listen to yourself and work with what you possess alone, how do you get to the ultimate of what's destined for you? Is the level of your thinking enough? Where does that confirmation come from if you only have what you believe within yourself to measure it by? We should always try to position ourselves to live a life that gives us complete fulfillment. The positioning could begin with listening. Listening to what the spirit within you is trying to usher out of you in an attempt to walk you into your best life.

Philippians 2:13; For God is working in you, giving you the desire and the power to do what pleases him.

My Prayer for you:
I know we all get to a point where we feel like we aren't as adequate as we may need to be in specific areas of our lives, especially when we attempt to approach a task unfamiliar to us. You must know that if God leads to it He will see you through it, if it's in accordance to His will for your life. It's only natural to experience some mixed emotions when deep within yourself, you can't phantom conquering such. You can. Anything you feel strongly enough for can be accomplished. It's usually within the depths of yourself that holds you back or releases the go ahead. I pray you receive all the power which is already in you to meet those goals and live out that dream. You are the one who makes the choice and no one can make it for you. I pray you embrace the positive motivation that allows your creativity to surface and enable you to push through feeling inadequate towards whatever it is you desire in life and may your faith be increased to get you there. Go for it.

DAY 15

That Fake Panel of Judges

For in the same way you judge others, you will be judged, and with the measure you use, it will be measured to you.
Matthew 7:2

Fake: A worthless imitation passed off as genuine.

Panel: A group of persons selected for some service.

Judge: One who forms an opinion or reach a conclusion through reasoning and information.

There are always going to be those individuals who feel they've been specifically selected to not only judge you, but also your previous and current circumstances; how you should feel, how you could have handled things better and especially what you could have done to prevent being incarcerated. Is anyone's opinion of what you've already done even relative to what you're facing today? You're already incarcerated for it. The main focus needs to be, what now! What needs to be done to begin living free from within and gaining sustainability after being released?

Personal Reflection:
Let's be real about something, people are going to be who they are. Please receive that and be aware of those who act like they're for your success and a 2nd chance. Some people will make it their unwarranted business to run down your entire life and state how ALL you needed to do was to go church, read the Bible, attend Sunday school and go to Bible study. Don't get me wrong, I'm in no way saying that your belief in a higher power is not a major component, but there is still work that needs to be done.

There is a "church" on just about every corner in the neighborhood I reside. So it used to make me wonder if one church is better than the other, if the Word was truer in one church than another or if so many people just feel they've received the call to preach and head a separate church. Some churches have 5 members and some have 3000 members. What's the difference? There is no perfect church anywhere. I've been to both smaller and larger. You'll embrace what moves your spirit. It's the commitment to the relationship between you and your higher power that will activate a spirit of discernment to determine where it's most spiritually motivational for you or not. Christians can be just as messy and non-Christians. I pray you never experience coming out of church feeling worse than when you went in because of the way people treated you, the way they sized you up because of what kind of shoes you didn't have on or the label that's not on your outfit or pocketbook. I'm not suggesting you deserve some form of special treatment, but because people are who they are there will always be those who simply feel you are not worthy of receiving another chance, as if they have a say in regard to placing you in heaven or hell.

The piece you're personally responsible for is also a major contributor to letting go of the past and moving forward. Your spiritual belief is definitely needed for you to draw strength from. The more intimate the relationship becomes, the more understanding you'll receive and you'll begin to embrace the internal freedom that comes from addressing those deep-rooted issues. The feelings associated with those issues will begin to be lifted creating an unchaining effect of your past. Those devastating and life altering experiences won't just magically disappear, but the way you've previously responded to that pain will definitely change for the better. Your previous thought process becomes healthier along with a renewed belief of new possibilities.

Positive results will not just materialize when you get released from jail or prison. Employment won't come in the mail, housing will not always simply present itself, and the possibility of you regaining custody of your children doesn't just happen. However; as I stated early on, everything does happen for a reason. When your relationship with the power in you that's greater than you are in place, you will definitely receive renewed strength to carry out whatever needs to be for your life. You'll receive increased confidence to push forward in whatever you need and blessings of what you want will materialize if that is part of the plan for your life. We may not receive all of what we want. That may not be what's best for you and or in line with the purpose planned specifically for you.

Unchained

Although our repentance gives us forgiveness, that doesn't necessarily mean you automatically get what you ask for.

Suggestions are one thing, but to ridicule you, degrade you and treat you as if you are less than part of the human race is unacceptable behavior. Securing oneself in passing judgement that lacks compassion towards people who do not have the ability to position themselves to come out of brokenness does not present as a part of a solution, but it actually is a major factor which is a systematic problematical entity in society's ignorance to what is a contributor to recidivism in a large portion of re-offenders.

Some individuals in positions of authority lack the concept that people who break the law, end up in jail, get out, then reoffend are just menaces to society. The issue is bigger than that. Are many willing to take that concept and turn it into a positive, absolutely not? There are some who place a monetary return as a higher regard for keeping someone incarcerated rather than investing in the renewal of unhealthy mindsets to prevent repeated incarcerations. I'm not trying to justify nor excuse someone for breaking the law, I'm trying to increase awareness that the problem is deeper than the surface of what's seen.

If a person gets released from jail, there are so many odds against them because they now have a label, "felon". There are so many employer's/business owners who refuse to employ individuals because of such. The mindset becomes, "Oh, they may steal from me". Do you realize how many people are currently at organizations stealing from the employer, they just haven't been caught? There is more criminal behavior taking place with people who haven't been caught as opposed to people who are trying to get back on track. It's not everyone, I get that. But how are people supposed to position themselves to get it right if all the doors are being shut in their faces. You can barely work anywhere, you experience difficulty living anywhere, and you can't receive this or that. There are many who do not want to return to their previous places of residency in an effort to prevent being in the same type of atmosphere thus reverting to the same type of lifestyle. It's what they know, it's their method of survival. Some women require the nurturing they've never received. The social skills never learned as well as other skills to create healthier mindsets. They require support, from the inside out.

Are we, as a society, more interested in labeling these individuals as opposed to strengthening our communities by rehabilitating the citizens who reside in them? I'm not stating that there's no one who has a genuine interest in providing support to the incarcerated, so please don't be insulted if you are a person or agency who does. Those "judges" are people who try to pick apart everything a person says to validate themselves and how much of a contributor they are, but really aren't. Someone who has not had such a pleasant or fairytale past, but is now living differently and believes if they can do it, everyone can do it. You can, but everyone's process is different. You have so many individuals who use their new found religious status to suppress their pasts, but in fact that past still remains. People have distinctive pasts with diverse feelings associated with that past and what works for one or some, does not work for everyone, I get it. If you do not actually process those entities that have caused your brokenness, it's basically suppressed baggage anchored with the hope of the feelings associated with it not ever surfacing. If it were just that simple, would there be recidivism if everyone that was incarcerated completed serving their sentence, turned to religious practices and never actually processed those issues? Many people do not go to the "root" of where the dysfunction began to form. The spirit of God gives us the strength to embrace our past along with any emotional difficulty which may arise with that healing process. Our faith gives us the belief that it will be done. We have to do our part of the process for it to all work together.

My prayer for you:
I pray you receive true freedom. First internally, then externally. May you realize how your purpose in life required that absolute truth. Broken people can relate to the "genuine you", not attempting to sugar coat your past. They need to hear it. When you verbalize your truth and are walking in your purpose, a spirit is presented that spreads the intended hope

to the broken. May your understanding be greatly increased. My prayers go up for you to not just accept, but to receive the divine plan prepared only for you.

Amen

DAY 16

Perfect love does not come until the first grandchild.
~Welsh Proverb

Love is the greatest gift
that one generation can leave to another
~Richard Garnett

For The Love of My Grandmother

Well reported of for good works; if she has brought up children, if she has lodged strangers, if she has washed the saints' feet, if she has relieved the afflicted, if she has diligently followed every good work.
1 Timothy 5:10

Grandmother: The mother of one's father or mother.

Knowledge and openness has given me the ability to understand why and how my family is the way it is today. Where a person comes from can be such a determining factor as to where they may end up, how they view specific issues and the manner in which they respond. A true sense of receptiveness and comprehension of all the entities involved also enables a person to break negative generational patterns which may cause one to not walk in their full potential of what's destined for them.

Personal Reflection:
My grandmother and I were always close. It only seemed natural for her to come live with me instead of going to a nursing home. I've been in the nursing field for 30 years and I knew what was needed to care for her. It was at that time I was able to learn much more about our family before her Dementia progressively worsened. She more often than not remembers who I am because she sees me daily, not so much my face or our relation, but my name. A lot of things began to unfold and I was provided a tremendous amount of information that provided more understanding of my family's dynamics and breakdown. The more she revealed, the more I was prompted to ask. I learned my grandmother's life was full of dysfunction and very few, if any, of her unresolved issues trickled down into how she raised her children. You cannot teach something you don't know. I believe with parenting, you do what you know to do, with what you have knowledge of and pray for the best for the rest. We have to make a conscious decision to become unchained from what keeps us from living our best life with clarity and wisdom while receiving the manifestation of our

Unchained

purpose for which that preparation took place. We can choose to ignite that internal power that will give us the courage to paralyze the negative influence those entities have on us.

It's very disheartening to see how divided my family is today. The form in which interactions take place have a high possibility of a shift in the way they proceed, but unfortunately many have rejected that shift and lost the connection.

My family is a prime example of how the past can affect the future of the generations to follow. When brothers and sisters who don't speak to one another have children, those children grow up being distant from their aunts, uncles and cousins. The cycle continues that way for generations to come, it simply gets repeated.

For me, my grandmother is where it all began. The majority of the issues within my family stem from that point and I learned about some of my grandmother's past and the abuse that occurred in her life. I began to see how a spirit can be transferred from one generation to the next. I also experienced how the lack of knowledge she had in regards to effective parenting was also transferred to the generations that followed. Again, we cannot teach what we don't know. She did what she knew how to do. She didn't know how to change what she did not know wasn't being effective or even the possibility of it not creating a well-roundedness in her children. The ones most affected don't even know how much of an impact it has on them, how they themselves are anchored in the pain or what they sow into their children, their relationships and lack thereof. Today, those feelings are ever-present in their interactions and the detachment of other family members. A few of them are holding onto the lack of nurturing, the feeling of not being protected and unpleasant experiences which occurred while they were growing up and they're now in their 50's & 60's. Their pain is deep, toxic and disadvantageous. If an openness and willingness to receive a way to let go of the hold it has on them doesn't occur, releasing that hold, moving forward in peace with themselves and others in the family cannot take place. The personal strongholds have created dysfunction in my family, but the healing can't take form without the first step of acknowledging, "It happened, I don't know how to talk about it and I don't know how to let it go!"

One would think a crisis would bring a family closer together, but the hold is so strong that even in my grandmothers' illness of Dementia, Alzheimer's and mental illness, they're even more distant from one another. She has children that live in less than a 4-mile radius who don't even bother to see her regularly. They're not employed. They haven't reached a point in their lives where letting go is an option or even a consideration. Their belief in how they personally choose to handle their relationships and interactions with the family are what's safe and healthiest for them. Fifteen hours per year of visits and phone calls is what it rounds out to per person closest to where my grandmother lives. It's sad, but accurate. I never want to experience the feelings I'd be consumed with had I not did what I could for her at this deteriorating time in her life.

She'll be 84 years old on June 27th, and all that she has been to me in my life is what I'm holding on to. Those things she didn't do right are nothing I want to cherish. She gave life to my mother who gave life to me and without her existence, I would not be here. I'm responsible for what I become in my life. With and without what was sown into me. We get to an age where we cannot blame others for where we are or aren't with ourselves internally and we can even accept and forgive the part they may or may not have played, but ultimately, we must become personally accountable of ourselves. Choosing to hold onto the past can be considered an easier way out of being accountable by blaming someone else for, "I can't, I won't, and I'm done!"

The detestation is so thick that it won't allow any beginnings for renewal. My cousins only do as their parent(s) do, if there is no exemplification of unconditional love, devotion or family connection, how would the example exist, how do we move forward, we don't. We actually grow further apart. We become more distant in our relation, thus expanding and creating a stronger generational separation and disconnect.

I don't believe in any way that this occurs only in our family, it's happening in many families today and has been for many years. It is a very sad vision as well as disheartening to see and there's nothing that one person can do. A joint effort has to take place for the cycle to change.

I truly understand and have experienced feeling inadequate in capacities of my life because I felt like I lacked pertinent knowledge in areas that were most vital in becoming the woman I was supposed to be. The reality in it all, is that I am the woman I am supposed to be. My journey to it was one which may appear to be the non-traditional route, but I have come full circle with how it was destined for me to arrive. All of the experiences in my life have been contributors to what was to be. I realize I can only answer for my own personal actions and not those of others.

My prayer for you:
I pray you embrace and utilize your past and current experiences to uplift yourself and accept it is all a part of the plan for your purpose. I pray you realize circumstances in life don't happen to hold you back, but that's it's a preparation for you to walk and succeed in what you will sow into others with what

you've experienced. You are an overcomer! You are destined for greatness because of the storms you've endured. I pray you release any titles you're refusing to release of being a victim and receive you've learned and lacked all involved for a divine purpose. Not to hurt you but to create in you the best you. You have what it takes and you are worthy.

Amen

DAY 17

My Brother, My Rock

A friend loveth at all times, and a brother is born for adversity.
Proverbs 17:17

Brother: A male having the same parents as another or one parent in common with another.

Rock: One that is similar to or suggestive of a mass of stone in stability, firmness, or dependability.

I have only one brother. Our past hasn't always been what it should have been. The abuse I've endured caused me to be a very angry girl growing up, but for as long as I could remember my brother has always been there for me. If not in my presence, definitely in my heart.

Personal Reflection:
The entire time while growing up, it has only been my brother and I. Although he always calls me old, I'm only three years older than he is. I used to fight so

much when I was in junior school and when my brother began attending junior high, my reputation for fighting paved a way for him to be quite popular. People referred to him as "Charlotte's brother."

My brother had moved to Virginia long before I decided to come. He had convinced me that the cost of living here was so much better than the prices I was paying in Bridgeport, Connecticut. I was working at a bank that was merging with another one and if I remained until the end, they would grant a decent severance package. I moved my belongings to VA and put them in storage and my daughter stayed with my brother for a few months. I returned to Connecticut until the bank closed and I then permanently relocated to VA and stayed with my brother and his family until I moved into my own apartment with my daughter.

It would be a few years before the relationship between my brother and I would blossom and bond the way it is presently. Kenny is not the type of brother who would interfere with my personal affairs and I didn't share too much of what my relationships entailed. It wasn't until this last marriage that he knew a part of my past that he more than likely heard of, but not so much in detail. He had become such a rock as this abusive and unstable relationship came to a close. He offered sound advice without being invasive. He gave it to me straight and didn't sugar coat it. I didn't need criticism or to be put down. He gave it to me exactly how I needed it. When there's no father figure in your life, the pouring of a male positive influence needs to come from somewhere and I'm grateful to have a brother who gained the wisdom over the years to have been there for me in the capacity in which he was. It was my brother who helped me realize that I managed to marry three of the same exact men. Although the behaviors were different, they were similar. I was able to see that it wasn't them, it was me. It was something in me that was attracted to their characteristics that was familiar to all of what I knew. My brother allows me to take a look at things from a different perspective and he gives me a sense of protection. Someone who looks out for my best interest and is not afraid to tell me what needs to be said. He has become my cognitive portion when my thinking can suddenly detour to the left; he aides in bringing me back to where I need to be.

We all need that person of strength who helps to keep us grounded and will keep it real without judging or degrading. He's a person who won't spare my feelings by saying what I want to hear, but does it with sincere love and compassion because of his strength and wants to genuinely see me succeed not only in my life, but with my vision. He is proud of me and unconditionally offers his assistance in whatever I need. Always there when I least expect it, but always right on time.

We decided to begin trying to bring the family together by having a Sunday Family Dinner. We plan what we're going to eat and everyone brings a dish. We do it every other Sunday and it was going very well for a while. Everyone is not as consistent, but my brother and I are always there. The company of family also does well for my grandmother, so whether everyone shows up or not we still have a great time, even though he and I talk just about every day.

I'm so grateful for where my relationship is with my brother and the bond couldn't have come at a more perfect time. This is such a very pivotal time in my life and I truly need someone I can always trust, which is my brother. In the good and the bad, who can I count on, my brother. Whether I'm right or off beat, who is always there, my brother.

I love you Kenny

My prayer for you:
I pray that you all have or embrace a person who is so true to you. Someone who will always keep it real so you are able to grow into your best you. I pray you always use your best judgement toward who you believe is trustworthy in your life and ensure you cherish, protect and respect that trust. My prayers for the strength you will definitely need to armor yourself against those entities not for you. There may be times when many experience not getting along with our siblings, but they are a part of you. I pray you find it in the depths of your being to forgive, whether you were right or wrong and move forward. So much time passes us by when we go lengths of time not speaking to one another, not visiting each

other and not being a part of our nieces and nephews lives. Having forgiveness will move you to places you could never imagine. Let it go and be a part of something truly wonderful. Don't allow next generations to only know you through a picture or hearing your name if you're alive to be with them.

Amen

DAY 18

When something bad happens, you have three choices.
You can either let it define you, let it destroy you,
or you can let it strengthen you.
~Kimberly Colburn

Living Free From Abuse

Love is patient and kind; love does not envy or boast; it is not arrogant or rude. It does not insist on its own way; it is not irritable or resentful; it does not rejoice at wrongdoing, but rejoices with the truth. Love bears all things, believes all things, hopes all things, endures all things.
1 Corinthians 13:4-7

Free: Not under the control or in the power of another; able to act or be done as one wishes.

Abuse: Abuse is any action that intentionally harms or injures another person.

We all have choices and decisions we're faced with. That road of decision making can at times take us for the most distraught whirlwinds of our lives simply because we don't always know which to decide. Do we make a decision based on what's best for ourselves or what we feel is best for others? Believe it or not, we do sometimes have the interest of others come to mind before what's the best decision for us.

Personal Reflection:
I've too often made decisions that would make someone else appeased rather than myself. Making others happier than I ended up in the long run had I made that specific choice for myself. Although I had to learn to choose myself in many instances; unfortunately, the hard way, I feel I've finally gotten to point in my life where I have to come first. I had to learn to not be a woman who found happiness only in pleasing someone else.

Considering myself to be a strong woman today, I know I wasn't as strong as I needed to be in certain areas of my life and protecting my heart in regards to being in a relationship. I overlooked too many things and tolerated even more. As I look back at the many things I put up with that I know I shouldn't have, today I don't become as overwhelmed in regrets as I do in celebrating my achievements. The accomplishments I've reached in living a life that began with abuse at such an early age, but how I also immersed in abusive relationships into my adult years; not one, but several. It seemed like I was a magnet for dysfunctional, disrespectful, broken and dishonest men. It is what it was but it isn't any longer.

I have survived them all. A broken heart and a shattered self-worth, I've managed to arrive to a place in my life where all of what I've experienced and use it not just for my good, but for the good of others. I had to realize and accept the fact that although I had a broken heart, it kept beating. I was tired of feeling as though I was failing and falling, exhausted with feeling like I was not amounting to anything. I felt used up with nothing left of me. Even with the many attempts to find a way to dig myself out of the pit I had put myself in, I couldn't.

It was such an extensive period of time before I realized how much stronger I was made along the way. As long as I was alive, I could keep trying. I had the determination to get it right. I had to ask myself, "How could I have felt used up with nothing left of me if I didn't even know who I was?" Knowing who I am and surviving all that I have been through was the preparation I needed to sow into the brokenness of others. What I've been through couldn't be the end. How I've handled and what I've done with what I've been through is where I had to arrive. I was equipped and called to serve in the capacity in which I do.

I recognize that there are so many people from all walks of life who've experienced so much more trauma than I have and then some whom haven't survived a fraction of what I have. Abuse is abuse, no matter how you look at it, nor how extensive it was. There's no way to look lightly at it. It affects each individual differently, and each person handles it the best way they know how or not at all.

Don't lose yourself in your bad experiences. As broken as they may cause you to feel, don't ever give up hope that you are worthy of a life free from abuse. Do your work on yourself to find out where it began to enable you to understand where the brokenness began? Go through the healing process. Yes, you will experience some pain, but it will pass. You know you can't go on like you have, and if you've convinced yourself that you can, you've only become complacent in that pain. You're not free. Until you release the source of your pain associated with your brokenness, it will just linger around awaiting its opportunity to re-surface in your next relationship. It's almost impossible to have a deep, honest, meaningful and whole relationship when you're attempting to genuinely love someone at the surface of pain. It will always be there until you confront it and release it.

My prayer for you:
I'm truly praying for your amazing leap out of the old you into the new and prepped for healing you. I pray you realize how strong you actually are and use that strength to free yourself from your own incarceration within yourself. I pray you embrace the Holy Spirit which will fill you with peace and comfort during this breakthrough you've been needing for so long. Prayers for a renewed mindset full of humbled gratefulness. I'm praying for success on your new path as walk in your purpose.

Amen

DAY 19

---

*Peace is not merely a distant goal that we seek
but a means by which we arrive at that goal.*
~*Martin Luther King, Jr.*

Choosing Peace

If possible, so far as it depends on you, live peaceably with all.
Romans 12:18

Choosing: To decide on a course of action, typically after rejecting alternatives:

Peace: Freedom from disturbance; quiet and tranquility.

During one's lifetime, there may be numerous questions about your life that can exist without an explanation or understanding. We may never have an answer to certain questions that we feel are causing us to have an emptiness within. We must make it an absolute necessity to move on and choose to have peace with the possibility of never having a resolution.

Personal Reflection:
As you've read in the previous essays, my family is extremely dysfunctional. It's not a putdown or as

though I'm trying to degrade them, it just it what it is. When I try to inquire about my past or our family history, I'm rarely given any clarity. You can talk to various members of the family and ask questions until the end of time, and it result to absolutely nothing. There are various versions of what could be the truth, but when you know who you're dealing with, you kind of get a clue that it's not necessarily the truth. Some even lie because they want to be so relevant. I can't force anyone to tell me what I want to know or even the truth about what I'm asking. There's a lot of speculation and when I try to make sense of it all, some things just don't add up. There's a lot of blaming, finger pointing or questionable statements made which left me dumb-founded.

I attempted to gain an understanding of why a lot of the decisions I've made in my life. I know much of it came from the unhealthy development from being molested, but I knew that wasn't the only interruption of my life. I'm a firm believer that spirits can be passed from generation to generation. I wanted to understand how it began and with whom. I also felt strongly about there being some generational curse since most of the women in my family appeared to be broken.

I had reached my end with the abusive relationships. I had been married to my last abusive husband and vowed it would not happen again. I've been on a hiatus from dating and definitely another relationship, for now at least. I had to make my life all about me and be on a mission to do things differently by working on the core of myself. It wasn't that difficult in the beginning because I was so bitter and angry in regard to the relationships going sour. I had never actually been single this long. The way it usually went was before the previous relationship was over there was already someone else I was seeing towards the end and we just moved on from there.

Spending this time with myself, getting to know me, learning and exercising what changes I needed to make within myself in order for this cycle to end. The relationship I needed to really improve was the one with God, who I knew would lead me exactly where He planned for me all along. I kept choosing a man for myself and always chose wrong. There was root to my choosing, and in a quest to live a mentally and emotionally healthier life with myself, there was some work I had to do. I couldn't just sit around and wait for the man that's going to be just for me and good to me without preparing myself to receive him. It's insane to not take a personal inventory of what internal enhancements I need to make within myself and actually expect to know when the right man has arrived. Without doing so, I believe I'd overlook that person because my mindset would be the same so how could I possibly choose differently and better.

At this moment in my life, I have more peace than I've ever had. I've accepted there's no longer a need to search to find out any additional information about my family tree than what I've already found out. I'm choosing to not be that person who makes it a lifelong feat to attain every single bit of information there is to know. I've accepted the purpose for my life and there's much more satisfaction in living for excellence in the plan for my life.

I've chosen peace. I've found the root of what I needed to know in order for me to be satisfied internally. I'm settled with peace within myself and the vison I have for my organization. There is so much fulfillment in me whenever I empower other women in correctional facilities who are experiencing brokenness. I keep my family in prayer that they too find the root to their brokenness and remove the toxicity within themselves so they'll be able to live a life of total peace. Not addressing their personal issues, but choosing to simply not interact with certain family members isn't healing, it's choosing to not face it. Their brokenness is illustrated in their behavior. People who spend more time talking negatively about other family members demonstrate an inability to really see their own issues. They want to hype themselves up as being issue free and everybody else has the problem. They want to prevent any attention to the fact that they too have a need for direct focus on what requires to be purged within themselves. People are going to talk about you whether you're doing great things or nothing. Choose to let me them talk, but your responsibility is to maintain focus on the path you've been prepared for. There's no guarantee we'll ever become a close knit family as we were once upon a time, whether it was genuine or not back then, it seemed like it was.

When you choose peace in your life, it's absolutely remarkable how you can choose to accept what you do and don't know about your past; you can humbly release any ill feelings that were a direct result from such. You're able to forgive easily and love unconditionally. You find yourself quick to reject any and everything that doesn't promote or stand for positive growth and emotional stability.

Don't spend your life trying to save others who don't feel there's a need to address internal dysfunction, it's enough trying to save yourself. Choose you and what is good and healthy for you. Make the choice to not keep secrets about your life that are damaging to your being able to move forward. Release those entities that hinder your growth and live. Have faith in the power greater than you to give you the courage needed to internally assess yourself and determine the areas within you that are anchoring pain from your past.

Unchained

My prayer for you:

I pray you find all the happiness for yourself that you deserve. I pray you choose peace over pain, peace over dysfunction, peace over sorrow, peace over molestation, peace over rape, peace over victimization, peace over grief, peace over everything in your past that you rejected which was meant to strengthen you and definitely peace over the enemy's attempt to keep you speaking and behaving negatively towards all of it.

Amen

DAY 20

Surviving without Support

And though a man might prevail against one who is alone, two will withstand him—a threefold cord is not quickly broken.
Ecclesiastes 4:12

How long have you felt as though you had to make this journey on your own? How many times have people vowed to be by your side, yet, you found yourself standing alone? After a multitude of letdowns, we make the choice to not count on anyone because we've been disappointed time after time and we refuse to let anyone else in. It's a choice to refuse support from anywhere. We sometimes possess such a negative aspect of those want to be a supportive entity in our lives, that we reject them all. Trust is something we choose to do. Your higher power will activate a spirit of discernment to determine who is genuine and who is not.

Personal Reflection:

I've learned over the years how so many people will act like they're for you and everything that you stand for, but actually are not. I've had my share of letdowns, but I made a choice to persevere through it all. I couldn't do it on my own. Initially I thought I could because I was too embarrassed to tell anyone all that I had been through. I was ashamed of what they would think of me. I was scared that if I had revealed my past, it would be used to judge me. My last husband took everything about my past and threw it in my face when he became angry. He used it in an attempt to break me down, and for a while it did. Over time what ended up happening is, a shift took place. I accepted what I had been through and began to use it for my good. When I told it, I had received the emotions associated with it differently. I spoke my truth. I spoke it over and over again when I started doing the groups in the correctional facilities. It started to become easier. I spoke it until I became free of the feelings associated with it which was actually beating me down. I allowed the spirit of God to work through me, and before I knew it, the anxiety disappeared, the fear was removed and victory was swarming through me.

I had to surround myself with people who were also victorious over their past circumstances. I began sowing positive affirmations into myself to keep me lifted. I began reading the Bible more to gain a perspective of the promises of God to keep that peace I was experiencing. I realized I didn't have to do it by myself and I couldn't survive it on my own. Yes, I fall short in areas of my life, probably more often than not, but my heart is clear and free to love and forgive.

I never thought I could love people I didn't even know because I never knew what unconditional love was. I grew to understand what it was when I made the decision to heal and started to answer the call which I was prepared for; sowing hope into the brokenness of incarcerated women.

We liberate one another during the group. It's the most empowering feeling to take what you've been through and share it with others who are experiencing the same or a similar type of pain. The women create a Sistahood where they empower one another. They've developed the understanding that if you become incarcerated with one mindset and you don't do a thing to renew your mindset, you ultimately return to the community with the very same mindset. What are you going to do differently? What have you learned to do differently? Chances are, you'll return to jail. More often than not, you will continue to hang around the same people who can't wait to celebrate your being home, in the same environment doing the very same things you were doing before.

What you've actually done is missed your opportunity to learn the lesson in your being incarcerated. The reality is, you will continue to go through it until you get the lesson you were supposed to get before you're able to move forward to the next challenge that's ahead of you created to make you stronger. These challenges are created to position you to live in your purpose. You're being prepared for it. Only you can make the decision to confront what's before, and that does require you going into your past.

We should have a system of support to help us survive, to help us get through the rough patches, and also to celebrate our accomplishments. A good friend is a good listener. We always need to vent. Not to put everyone in your business, but to hear yourself saying what's on your mind. We can sometimes figure out what we need to do in certain situations, speaking out loud makes it real. You make a choice to handle it on own, but the great thing is, you don't have to. Surround yourself with like-minded or more advanced people attempting to meet goals and live their best life. The energy from those types of individuals brings a calmness to what may seem to sound like chaos inside your head.

Believe me, I know all about thinking you had someone you thought you could trust and they totally disappointed you. It's not the end of the world and it doesn't stand for never being able to trust anyone under any circumstances whatsoever for the duration of your life. You can trust again although it may take a minute. Don't categorize everyone as being the same. Again, it's a choice we make to do or not to do certain things.

We are all beautiful survivors. We still have power within ourselves, and that power which remains within us is to be used. No matter how many times we get knocked down, we're not out and don't count yourself out. We need to use what we have for greater things and not to destroy ourselves internally. Don't you know you have what it takes? You do. Step out of the old damaged you and into what is to become of you silently awaiting your grand arrival.

My prayer for you:
I'm sending love to you. I'm sending prayers for abundant Blessings on you. I'm praying for the release of any and everything within you that shouldn't exist to be released. I'm praying you embrace your beauty and your power. I'm praying anyone who has a guard up from trusting allows the layer to be peeled back to allow a spirit of love to flow steadfastly within you.

Amen

DAY 21

You are Enough

*"But you are a chosen race, a royal priesthood, a holy
nation, a people for his own possession, that you may
proclaim the excellencies of him who called you out of
darkness into his marvelous light."*
I Peter 2:9

How many can attest to the fact that at times, with
everything you've been through, you felt you just
weren't enough? With all the bad decisions we've
made, knowingly and unknowingly we couldn't
manage to put one thought in front of the other and
come up with a logical reason why we weren't moving
forward and doing great things with our lives. Been
there, done that. Now it's time to stop. It's time to
stop thinking so little of ourselves and trust while
believing we are destined to live a life most fulfilling
of all we desire within His will for us.

Personal Reflection:
I never dreamed of being in the place of my life I am at this present moment. Writing a book? I thought about it a long time ago, but I hadn't reached a point where I actually thought I'd do it. And now, here it is. Back when I had the thought of it, I did not have had all I'm sowing into you like I am now. I had not reached the point of acceptance, understanding of the lessons I had to go through, reality, compassion, forgiveness, unconditional love, healing or even ministry.

I really had to go through storm after storm to get here. When I thought I wasn't enough, my relationship with God had to get real before I would actually understand what it is that He wanted me to do, what the purpose for my life is. It was as though my entire ability to quietly listen, understand and be obedient to what was tugging at me. I stated earlier that I was never a speaker, I was so shy and petrified to speak in front of people. I never felt like I actually had anything of importance to speak to people about. I was going through life, but not understanding why

I was going through all the events taking place in my life.

Believe it or not, my last husband suggested it to me, and I took off. It just made sense. I wasn't even hesitant about doing it especially because it came from him, but God will use other people to point you in the right direction. It didn't necessarily mean we were meant to remain together, but I actually had to go through that relationship with him. Getting out of it made me stronger than I've ever been in my life, and it was time. It was time to move forward and begin using all I've experienced to sow hope into others so they'd know if I can be brought out of it, they can as well.

It was as though God waited for me to get it together and as soon as I accepted the assignment, my purpose was born. He had been preparing me the entire time, but because I wasn't receiving the lessons in what I was going through, I kept going through them, sound familiar? You keep doing the same things with the same mindset. You keep getting involved with the same types of people because you're either not making an attempt to want to do something

Unchained

different about the way you keep feeling, you've convinced yourself that your current life is all there is and that's what you deserve, you don't know how to change, or you could very well be hearing it, and the complacency of being broken has caused a comfort zone to make you ignore it.

As soon as you cease the fight in you, you will experience some peace. The fight is not even yours but you refuse to give it up. Some people feel that is the only control they have over everything else, their pain. What we fail to realize is we are not in control of any of it, it's controlling us. I believe if we were simply the worst people, we would have been gone out of existence long ago. We remain for a reason, after everything we've been a part of, we are still here. When? When do we get tired enough to say, "I'm just so tired of fighting a battle I cannot win on my own.!"

My essays are written to bless you. To bless you in the mightiest way. To share with you what I've experienced in my life and how I came out of it. How you too can come out of those dark fearful places within yourself that have caused you to lose hope. I believe you have hope; we can't survive without it. It may be the tiniest amount, but if you're incarcerated and reading this book, there is something in you that wants better. You can have it, it's already in you. You just have to make a move in a different direction, and backwards isn't it.

My prayer for you:
I pray you take the time to connect with the higher power within you. I'm praying you get yourself to a point in your life where you begin to value your worth and trust there's a purpose planned specifically for you. We all have specific assignments because of the situations we've gone through. You bring your individuality to your assignment. I'm praying it flows through you with feelings you never thought you could ever possibly imagine. I'm praying for you. I want you to have peace no matter how much time you have to serve. Your time doesn't have to be hard time. God will use you right where you are. I'm praying you open up and allow it to take form in you. You have nothing to lose, but everything to gain. Give up the fight. I love you.

Amen

10 Gripping Facts about Women in Prison

Devlin, Mike "10 Gripping Facts About Women In Prison" 17 July 2004, www.listverse.com

The First Women's Prisons

Women's prisons are a relatively new concept. In the past, the rare female scoundrel was usually housed in a separate part of a men's facility. The first women's facility in the United States, Indiana Women's Prison, was built in 1869 and received its first prisoners four years later. The first federal prison for women would not follow for decades. The Federal Industrial Institution for Women was built in Alderson, West Virginia, where it opened on April 30, 1927.

It was a far cry from the hardscrabble penitentiaries of modern times, with practically nonexistent security and inmates put to work with clerical, cooking, and farming duties instead of being locked in cells 23 hours a day. The facility's stated goal was not to punish the inmates for the misdeeds but to reform them so they could become upstanding members of society. After all, most of these women were not black widow murderesses but girls who had fallen under the sway of drugs and alcohol during the Prohibition era.

The Exploding Incarceration Rate

The incarceration rate in the United States is something of an international joke. It's higher than that of any other nation in the world, including questionable regimes like Russia and China. But even among these astronomical numbers, the fastest-growing population of prisoners in the United States are women. Women's prisons didn't even exist two centuries ago, but today, there are over a million women in the criminal justice system.

The numbers are truly staggering. Between 1980 and 2006, the population of women in prison jumped 800 percent. The situation is even grimmer for minorities, who comprise two–thirds of all incarcerated women. Sadly, most women behind bars have been convicted of nonviolent crimes like drug possession or prostitution, and even violent offenders have

Unchained

heartbreaking stories. For example, up to 90 percent of women convicted of murdering a man were also abused by that man.

Giving Birth

No one deserves more tender loving care than a woman in labor, but incarcerated women are prisoners first and mothers second. In 30 US states, they can be shackled down while giving birth, a step that has been condemned by the ACLU and various health organizations. Amnesty International has called it a violation of human rights. Binding a woman during labor presents a host of unique problems for the mother, child, and physician

Being born in prison isn't exactly the best start in life, but there are some success stories. Perhaps most notably, actress Leighton Meester, one of the stars of the show *Gossip Girl*, was born in a federal prison in Texas, where her mother had just begun a 10-year sentence for drug smuggling. Some states offer programs allowing mothers to care for their infants behind bars, generally reserved for nonviolent offenders with short sentences. The programs can extend from one month to three years and have shown unfailingly positive results.

Families Displaced

Sadly, many women behind bars were primary caregivers for their children. When they are locked up, families are left with few options. The lucky ones can be placed with relatives, but more often, the kids are sent to foster care. Many of these children are lost to their mothers forever. The federal Adoption and Safe Families Act, enacted in 1997, requires states to terminate parental rights to children that spent at least 15 of 22 consecutive months in the foster care system, freeing them up for adoption. The median minimum sentence for incarcerated women is 36 months.

Worse still, the comparative rarity of women's facilities means that they are often located so far away from home that it can be difficult, and sometimes impossible, for families to visit. Isolation from their loved ones does little to help prisoners' attitudes or reintegration with society.

Unchained

Death Row

Despite the meteoric rise in the population of women in prison, less than 2 percent of those on death row are women. In the last 200 years, the only woman sentenced to death for a lesser crime than murder was Ethel Rosenberg. She and her husband were convicted of treason for running a spy ring, providing the secrets of the atomic bomb to the Soviet Union. They were executed by electric chair on June 19, 1953.

Probably the most infamous female death row inmate was Aileen Wuornos, a Florida prostitute who murdered seven men in one bloody year between November 30, 1989 and November 19, 1990. She spent 10 years on death row before being executed by lethal injection on October 9, 2002. Her last meal request was for a cup of black coffee. Her last words were "Yes, I would just like to say I'm sailing with the rock, and I'll be back, like *Independence Day* with Jesus. June 6, like the movie. Big mother ship and all, I'll be back, I'll be back."

Healthcare

The massive influx of women in prison has left the system reeling, as facilities are woefully unprepared to attend to the unique health problems women face. Routine gynecological care and mammograms are often unavailable, meaning that women behind bars frequently succumb to diseases like cervical cancer, which is often successfully treated if detected by Pap smear in its earliest stages.

There is also a much higher incidence of substance abuse problems and communicable diseases like HIV and hepatitis C among women in prison than men, often due to a history of trading sex for drugs. Women are also more susceptible to a number of chronic conditions such as varicose veins, constipation, anemia, urinary tract infections, and migraines. They even outstrip incarcerated men in mental health issues, often being the victims of lifelong abuse. Sadly, the vast majority of women who are incarcerated fall well below the poverty line, and even before they were imprisoned, they had little to no access to healthcare.

Assault by Guards

In a perfect world, the guards and support staff at women's prisons would all be female. While this would hardly end all abuse, it would certainly alleviate many issues. Unfortunately, about 40 percent of guards in American women's prisons are male. In some states, that number climbs even higher. This means that abuses like beatings and rape are terrifyingly common.

One institution infamous for such activity is the Julia Tutwiler Prison for Women in Wetumpka, Alabama. An investigation indicated over one-third of its employees have had sex with inmates, often in exchange for basic commodities like cigarettes and toiletries. Although there are indications that Tutwiler is improving, it still frequently makes the shortlist of worst prisons in America. The federal government has stated that the circumstances there may be so bad as to be unconstitutional.

Orange Is the New Black

The first two seasons of the Netflix original series *Orange Is the New Black* were a runaway success, having been renewed for a third season. The story is based on the real life experiences of Piper Kerman, a well-educated middle-class woman. Kerman was an unlikely candidate to spend time in prison, but in her mid-twenties, she began laundering money for a West African drug kingpin. She was indicted five years later and eventually spent 13 months behind bars, starting in 2004. Motivated by the curiosity of others following her release, she penned *Orange Is the New Black: My Year in a Women's Prison.*

The bestselling memoir was adapted into the Netflix series to great critical acclaim. One of the many compliments the show has garnered is that it features well-developed characters rather than the stereotypical criminals who often fill such portrayals of the prison system. Among them is a transgender woman named Sophia Burset, who is played by transgender actress Laverne Cox. For flashback scenes portraying Burset's life before her transition, the show employs Cox's real-life twin brother.

These days, Kerman has moved away from the sordid underbelly of drug trafficking. She is a frequent

Unchained

public speaker and nonprofit activist, serving on the board of the Women's Prison Association.

Exploitation Films

Before *Orange Is the New Black*, movies and shows about women in prison took a decidedly different tack. They were more along the lines of soft-core porn and often featured themes of lesbianism, nudity, and cat-fighting. While such films truly hit their stride in the late 1960s, they date back to at least the early 1930s, with the release of 1931's *Ladies of the Big House* and 1934's *Ladies They Talk About*, which starred Hollywood legend Barbara Stanwyck.

The genre, called "women in prison" or "WiP," is popular in several countries, including the United States, Italy, and China. Several dedicated cinema guides to the genre are available, detailing such films as 1985's *Red Heat*. Starring a post-*Exorcist* Linda Blair, the film portrays the tribulations of an American woman captured by East Germans during the latter stages of the Cold War. Not surprisingly, in the age of hardcore pornography, the WiP genre remains prolific.

Women's Prisons around the World

While women's prisons in the Western world are hardly the sort of places you'd ever want to live, the conditions of such facilities are completely deplorable in other parts of the world. South Africa is home to some of the worst women's prisons in the world, described by a former inspector as "shockingly inhumane." Former prisoners have described scenes in which dozens of people are crammed into a cell with just one shower, sink, and toilet, leading to outbreaks of violence that guards are unable or unwilling to control.

Even in Greece, which is part of the European Union, conditions can be nasty. At Thiva Women's Prison north of Athens, vaginal canal searches are frequent, and those who refuse to succumb to the demeaning procedure are put into solitary confinement and plied with laxatives until it can be determined they aren't concealing anything. Although Greek prisons claim that such practices have been outmoded, they continue to be seen by visiting monitors from the European Committee for the Prevention of Torture.

Congressional Research Service Report

From a portion of a report submitted on June 1, 2011 by the Congressional Research Service, it states that over 95% of the prison population today will be released at some point in the future, and each year in the United States almost 650,000 offenders are released from prison. The Department of Justice's (DOJ's) Bureau of Justice Statistics (BJS) has estimated that two-thirds of all released prisoners will commit new offenses (recidivate) within three years of their release. Many studies have indicated that reentry initiatives that combine work training and placement with counseling and housing assistance can reduce recidivism rates.

Offender reentry includes all the activities and programming conducted to prepare ex-convicts to return safely to the community and to live as law-abiding citizens. Reentry programs are typically divided into three phases: programs that prepare offenders to reenter society while they are in prison, programs that connect ex-offenders with services immediately after they are released from prison, and programs that provide long-term support and supervision for ex-offenders as they settle into communities permanently. Offender reentry programs vary widely in range, scope, and methodology. The best-designed programs, according to the research in the field, are those that span all three phases.

A Government Accountability Office (GAO) report also suggests that post-release planning should begin as early as possible, ideally as soon as an inmate is admitted into prison or even immediately after sentencing. Such planning could include helping the offender to develop the skills and knowledge base necessary to find a well-paying job and have access to education, such as General Equivalency Degree classes for those who have not completed high school, and either vocational training or college classes for those that have completed high school but have not settled on a career.

As offenders approach their release date, the research suggests that reentry planning focus on connecting offenders with the community and workplace resources they will need to get established. Again, employment and access to education have been cited by many studies as two of the most important aspects contributing to the successful reintegration of ex-offenders into society.

Lastly, it is important for the reentry process to extend deep into the offenders' reintegration into society. Indeed, for many offenders, the first few weeks of adjustment after release are actually less difficult than the longer period of community reintegration. In many cases, this period of time can span the entire three to five years that offenders are sometimes supervised in the community.

James, Nathan, "Offender Reentry: Correctional Statistics Reintegration Into the Community and Recidivism," CRS Report for Congress, (June 1, 2011).

Letters from my Ladies of *WE1A*

The following writings were submitted by a few of the women who are currently and have previously participated in the Women Empowerment workshop at Hampton Roads Regional Jail, Portsmouth, VA; Virginia Peninsula Regional Jail, Williamsburg, VA & Western Tidewater Regional Jail, Suffolk, VA. They were overjoyed at the opportunity to be a part of something so positive, especially in their current situation. They were given two questions to answer to sow hope into you. They've been working on their inner self. Many leave jail and never return. They have found the source of where their pain began and why the decisions they've made resulted with incarceration. They were broken and made the decision to position themselves to become whole.

Some continue to still have work to do as far as their inner being. The answers to the questions given are your gift from the ladies to allow you to see how being provided a platform to put their feelings on, has increased their hope and self-esteem. They have positioned themselves to move forward and having a support system maintains a focus of successful transition whether they are released, going to a program or going to prison. A true sense of freedom within yourself will allow you to conquer any fear you may have in regard to living a successful life outside of a correctional facility. Not just existing, but actually living.

These are the two questions the women were given to answer;

1) Why did you begin taking the WE1A group at your facility?

2) How has taking the group empowered your inner being?

This is their message of hope to whomever reads this book. They send their Blessings to each of you.

To which ever lady has chosen to pick up this amazing book. My name is Paula S. I am 39 years old and my story began from age 9 until age 12 with being raped by my father and a mother who allowed it. I wasn't taught to be loved, how to love, how to be a mother, a sister, an aunt or grandma. Alcohol, drugs and men failed me enough. At only 82 pounds, I prayed for God to help me before it was too late. "Jesus take the wheel".

I met Ms. Williams and started WE1A. It was the beginning of the rest of my life. I now weigh 170 pounds with a sentence of 14 months in a maximum secure facility. I began to dig out the bad within me and sow in the good and now I love me some me.

Paula S., HRRJ

My name is Linda W. and I am 35 years old. For as long as I can remember, I have been in and out of abusive situations. I had a low self-esteem, no self-love, self-worth or self-respect. I needed to find myself. My history of abuse didn't allow me to know my true self.

WE1A has helped me overcome the abuse in my life. After joining the group, I have overcome areas that prevented me from moving forward. I recommend this group to any woman who is trying to overcome their past.

Linda W., HRRJ

I began attending the Women Empowerment group because of the pain I had from childhood. The two things that caused the most pain was being taken from my parents and raped at two years old.

Attending the group has helped me release my anger by allowing me to talk out those problems from my childhood and no one judges me.

J. Henderson, HRRJ

I attended the women empowerment group because I knew that I needed help working on some of my problems. It would help me to gain power over some things that have happened to me and help me be stronger.

It showed me to stop blaming everyone for what my downfalls are and start to own up to my wrong doings. To start standing on my own two feet and realize no one owes me anything. I need to be a woman of my word.

I began attending WE1A because I was tired. While talking to a friend, she told me how WE1A was a group that was like no other. It wasn't like your typical AA, NA, Anger Management or Thinking for a Change. This was group to help me get back to me, and that's what I wanted. I wanted a group that would help me get back to loving me.

Women Empowerment has helped me to take ownership of my "stuff". To stop looking for sympathy and a place to put blame but accept responsibility for myself and my actions. It has helped me to get to the root of a lot of my hurt and anger. To allow me a way to deal with those emotions in a safe and healthy way. To get the positive advice & constructive criticism needed to deal with and let go of those things that have been holding me back for so many years. WE1A has taught me it's ok to be a strong independent woman and love yourself.

Janelle W., HRRJ

I began attending the group with the intent of strengthening myself as a woman and mother. I had lost hope of what it is I'm here in life for because of my incarceration. I needed guidance, uplifting words and positive individuals around me in my time of need.

This group has built up my confidence of making better and wiser choices in life so that I may succeed. I have received the empowerment to excel in life and goals that I've set. I'm no longer afraid, I'm stronger and wiser and I know that "I will survive through it all".

A. Kelly, HRRJ

The inspiration I have gotten out of women empowerment is Sistahood and spiritual guidance. How to cope with emotional, physical and mental hurts I've had in the past.

How to come together as women to help lift each other up where we fall short in life. Also, how we can learn from each other's experiences with life struggles.

Anonymous, HRRJ

I joined the women empowerment group to help myself be able to share my feelings and talk about things that needed to be talked about.

The group has helped me express my feelings to people.

B. Bullock, HRRJ

I needed women empowerment! The name alone sold me. I felt I was in a good place where I could be open and start something positive that would be helpful to my growth and future.

It showed me someone besides God truly cares and loves me. Women period! Every group is a new exciting experience. When I'm in group it shows me that I am not alone, we're all dysfunctional and truly amazingly beautiful. I'm listening and learning. I have been able to share and release. I realized that I was only existing, not living. Every day is a new day and working on myself is something that I have to do continually. I'm getting better and I'm looking forward to my future. I'm very thankful for C. Williams for starting women empowerment. I look forward to being a part of women empowerment when I'm released. Thank you and I love you too.

M. Davis, HRRJ

I wanted to find a format where incarcerated women could get together, leaving the drama behind and discuss real issues that affect us in and out of jail. Hopefully finding people and topics to relate to. My biggest hope, to redefine myself and hopefully end the cycle that keeps bringing me back behind these doors.

It's helping me to see things that maybe I haven't wanted to deal with. Things I've avoided for a long time. I'm also learning that without forgiving myself I cannot move forward, that I'm setting myself up for failure by keeping this self-loathing mentality.

Anne F., HRRJ

I began attending the WE1A group to try and obtain tools to enable me to combat my addictions and character defects while in a confined setting. I wanted to gain self-confidence, self-love, and self-respect to myself and others alike. To break the family curse. Yes, I can begin to learn self-identity.

The group has helped me to dig down deep to the roots of my dysfunction and pain. It has also helped to identify my character defects. Moreover, it has given me hope to know that I am not alone and I can do this one day at a time. I am worth the time and worth being treated like a person.

"I can all things through Christ who strengthens me."
Philippians 4:13

S. Williams, HRRJ

I thought this was just a way out of the pod, but I soon found out that by completing the assignments, I was forcing myself to be honest about my flaws and faults. I was asked to look deeper than the surface and I knew I needed to make changes. It wasn't until now, just where I needed to start. I figured it would be about sharing sob stories but this class has forced me to open old wounds and start to repair myself at my most vulnerable stages/areas and rebuild the inner most parts of self that needed therapy. Supportive women have really become like sisters because I might be broken but I know I'm not the only one. I'm not alone and I am worth the love it takes to stay positive and move forward, free and happy.

This class has opened my eyes to why I have made some of the choices I have and how to address certain situations and predicaments in which I placed myself. It's helped me identify triggers which in turn helped me recognize what I need and how to go about getting it.

A. Ward, HRRJ

Honestly, I thought it would maybe stop some drama in the pod, help me take up some time. I didn't really know much about the class, I just wanted to help occupy my time. But after taking it, I will never miss a class. I've decided I love the class so much; I want to work for Ms. Williams one day! Actually, I will work for Ms. Williams one day.

The group has shown me that it is ok to be broken, I'm not destroyed. There is still a chance to fix myself.

Unchained

We as women need to lift each other up instead of bringing each other down. I am so strong. I am capable of so much. I am beautiful and I'm beginning to love myself for the first time in my life. It is possible to feel free on the inside even if you're not physically free. My body may not be free, HRRJ may be keeping me confined, but they can't confine my spirit. I control that and I'm deciding to set my spirit free because I've been a prisoner inside my head for too long. Enough is enough. Thanks to Ms. Williams, I'm working on freeing myself while being locked up. This is the closest to freedom I've ever felt in a while and it's all in my heart.

M. Eddiani, HRRJ

I went to my first class and I loved it. I never thought about joining any programs until after I was sentenced. I missed out on a year of amazing teachers, positive encouragement, a loving environment, spiritual motivation and a true blessing. I have received every Wednesday afternoon. But God has blessed me with this program. It truly gives me something to look forward to every week. When you're in jail, you have to find positives in every situation. You have to be willing to pull yourself up and open your mind and heart. Let go, let God.

This group has helped me find the deep down hidden, almost forgotten; lost, hurt and pain. That I need to be able to release to be able to see how I no longer want to be. Things I never even realized until much later that some of what I thought was just my past was still in my present. I am a better person for waking up to face this head on. Not just for me, but for my children and loved ones. You have to love God first, love yourself, be willing to fix yourself with God's help and everything will fall into place. I love coming to this group because it's not just another group, it's real...100%. Thank you WE1A! You are a true blessing.

T.R., HRRJ

I was in pain and in search of a way to stop the vicious cycle of recidivism in which I contributed to in my life. So I started a familiar path of "doing something with my time" while incarcerated and getting away from the madness of the jail dorm. I

joined WE1A not knowing I was gonna "meet me".
The WE1A staff helped me to break down the walls of
rejection I built against accepting my part in my own
self destructive behaviors by looking into the mirror
of my souls' reflection of my past, and present pains
and giving me hope for my future. I'm so grateful for
the WE1A sign-up sheet in the jail pod that I walked
away from many times before I signed it.

The group helped me by giving me the tools I needed
to cope with life inside the jail and after my release
from jail. When I had to face some of the same issues
that triggered a negative mind set which landed me
in jail numerous times. The support from my peers
and the WE1A staff were awesome as shared portions
of me.

Adrienne O., VPRJ

There I was back in the same situation that I had
been in so many times before. At the time I was 46
years old, struggling with a 20-year crack addiction.
I truly wanted out. I had already tried in-house
treatment (jail), NA, moving to different places and
even God! Nothing seemed to have kept me with

Unchained

minimum clean time and eventually picking up. While locked up this time, I kept having quite a few inmates talking about a group, "WE1A". I had absolutely nothing to lose, so I signed up for the group. After my first class, I knew that WE1A was going to be a part of my life.

I can remember asking Ms. Williams if I could speak with her privately. I mentioned to her that I wasn't going to be in jail long and I needed something with structure outside of those walls. I asked her how can I continue this group on the outside and would she be willing to be a part of my support team. This conversation took place in August 2014. I was released in February 2015 from Hampton Roads Regional Jail in Portsmouth, VA with plans to never return.

I continue to participate in the after-care support group at WE1A, NA and I've obtained a sponsor. I faithfully use the tools that I've acquired to refrain from ever using drugs. Today, I take care of my responsibilities by paying my fines, working a steady job, trusting the God of my understanding and I have even obtained a valid driver's license. I can sincerely

Unchained

testify that WE1A has been the foundation that set forth to my staying clean and also accomplishing the things that I have.

Tammy A., HRRJ

I began attending the women empowerment group because I wanted a better understanding of myself as a woman in this world so that I could teach and give my daughters, my granddaughter and the other women in my life how to become better women. I feel that this group could also help me find out what I need to do for myself.

This group has helped me to get a better understanding of myself and to know that I am loved, cared about and that somebody loves me and accepts me for who I am, 'The real me".

K. Williams, HRRJ

I actually didn't request the women empowerment group. I was put in the group. I am very grateful for the opportunity to be a part of this group and have the support of my classmates and Ms. Williams. There aren't many opportunities for women who are incarcerated to fix the underlying issues that brought us here, which is why I'm so appreciative of WE1A.

Since I started attending the women empowerment group, I have received understanding of why I do what I do.

Anonymous, WTRJ

The only reason I came the first time was to get out of the unit.

The reason I kept coming back, the instructor Mrs. Trudy. I felt like she really cares for what she was talking about. I felt like she cares about me. I've suffered a lot of tragedy in my lifetime. I felt comfortable in sharing. I've learned so much. This class is a true blessing to my life.

Laurie T., VPRJ

I began attending Women Empowerment when I was incarcerated at Hampton Roads Regional Jail back in July of 2016. I had personal issues I was dealing within myself. Having a roommate tell me about this class and how it has helped her made me think that this was something that I wanted to try. I started in the class and listened to other people and their stories. Upon the assignments that Ms. Williams gave allowed me to think about my past and why things were happening to me. I talked about my parents to even being raised by my grandparents. I didn't understand why things were happening to me until assignment after assignment pulled it out of me. I stayed in this class until I was released from incarceration. This class allowed me to get my spiritual as well as inner channel back to where I needed to be.

This group has helped me in many ways. It has allowed me to be more positive with myself and others. I know forgiveness will eventually come with the ones that I've hurt. I have apologized to my siblings and have become closer than I have ever been with them. I have a relationship again with my family that I never thought that I could recover. Even though the pain is still there work thru it and keep believing that one day that it

Unchained

183

will draw my family even closer. Even though I still deal with a lot of issues I still take it day by day and pray more. I ask God to show me the way and if it is in his will then let it be done. This group has also given me more self-esteem as well as forgiving others and don't mind speaking about my past.

J. James, HRRJ

I began attending the group with the intent of strengthening myself as a woman and mother. I have lost hope of what I'm here in life for because of my incarceration. So I need up lifting and individuals around me in my time of need.

This group has built up my confidence of making correct and wiser choices in my life so that I may succeed. I have received the empowerment to excel in the goals that I've set. I'm no longer afraid. I'm stronger and wiser and I also know "I WILL SURVIVE THROUGH IT ALL!"

A. Kelly, HRRJ

My personal message to you

Always remember that your present situation
is not your final destination
~Unknown

I've written for you 21 essays from my life. I've written them to share how amazingly your life can take a phenomenal shift when you make a decision to want better for yourself. How circumstances in your past are preparations for the purpose designed only for you. I pray that you receive how beautiful, influential and strong each of you are, with respect to all you've been through. You are champions within yourself and for your broken Sista's who are coming behind you, sow into them and use your strength to help another with your voice.

Celebrate and embrace one another instead of judging what we do and don't look like, what we have or lack. We come from different backgrounds and lifestyles. As women, we've come a long way. We must give ourselves the permission to heal and not silence our pain. We have a voice in our lives, choose

Unchained

to use it and free yourself. Don't shrink yourself to protect someone who mistreats you. You deserve the best of what's for you, and you won't be ready to receive what's best if you're not rid of those things which cause you to feel you have to settle. Your life is awaiting the wholeness of your arrival.

I have not attempted to blame or shame anyone in this book. It's my life, how I viewed my experiences, and the strength it took to overcome. It's my voice which I have total freedom to use, and my choice of how I want to use it. There is power not only in our life experiences, but also in the healing from those experiences and I pray you work towards yours. I pray for an overflow of healing within each and every one of you.

I love my family and although we're dysfunctional, my love grows even stronger and my prayers goes deeper. I now understand how it became that way and I've received and implemented how to not pass it to my next generation. I can only be responsible for the actions I make towards my own personal growth, but if what I've shared can possibly empower others whether within my family or somewhere else in the world, then so be it, my prayer is answered.

Don't give away what's freely given to you which is rightfully yours, your power. Everyone has their own and deny anyone from taking it away. Don't consume yourself with the issues of others, especially if you're in transition with your own. To get caught up in another persons' refusal to give themselves permission to heal, can reduce your capacity to heal within yourself and delay or cease moving forward in your life.

Don't suffer in silence. We make a choice to remain anchored in pain and anger. Although you may feel it's easier said than done, ask yourself if you're making a true and conscience effort to make the first step do so. Choose to be free and unchain yourself what from keeps you captive of your past. You have every right to be happy and at peace. You are worthy to be forgiven and unconditionally loved.

Unchained

Although everyone you may have wronged might possibly not forgive you, you keep moving forward. That's the part for which you are accountable for. You must strive to position yourself on the path destined by not only working out your own issues, but also using the power of God that's already within you. Others not forgiving your past has nothing to do with where you're going.

I love you, I believe in you and I pray the very best for you in all you do.

C. Williams
Unchained

Made in the USA
Columbia, SC
29 July 2017